Praise for
One Nation, Under Attack

"*One Nation, Under Attack* is an eyeopening, hard-hitting, factual, and well-documented representation of world events as they relate to Bible prophecy—as we count down the final hours to the return of Christ. Where is America in prophecy? What about China? Will the U.S. economy survive? *One Nation, Under Attack* takes on these questions and more. Grant Jeffrey—my dear friend, mentor, and colleague of more than twenty years—has gone home to meet the Lord, and our loss is heaven's gain. But I am sure you will agree that Grant's last book is also his best. Maranatha!"

—JACK KINSELLA, publisher and editor, Omegaletter.com

"Not only did Grant Jeffrey see the signature of God written across the pages of Scripture, but all of us who knew him could see the signature of God written across his heart, soul, and mind as he declared the gospel of Jesus Christ. Grant never hesitated to preach and teach the promise of Christ's coming and the message that Jesus alone can bring peace to a troubled soul and give you the hope of heaven."

—DR. ED HINDSON, dean, Institute of Biblical Studies,
Liberty University

"Heralding the premillennial revival, Grant perfected the art of the prophecy book in a way that no one had done before: spectacular new discoveries, cutting-edge research, timely subjects that weigh heavily on the public's mind. When Grant said Jesus was coming soon, we believed him! He was the voice of authority in the world of Bible prophecy. Grant affected millions of lives with his books and television ministry. Scholar, tireless researcher, mentor, friend. Grant's voice is one we came to trust and depend on."

—Bob Ulrich, editor, *Prophecy in the News*

"On a personal level I'm saddened that I'll not see Grant Jeffrey again on this earth. One of the world's great authorities on Bible prophecy about the end times, and one of the great warriors for the faith, has been withdrawn by the Lord. I rejoice that Grant is now face to face with the Lord. His burdens are over, his work is finished. I know we will miss the voice of Grant Jeffrey. But we shall all see him soon."

—Hal Lindsey, best-selling author and television host,
The Hal Lindsey Report

ONE NATION,
UNDER ATTACK

WaterBrook Titles by Grant R. Jeffrey

Fiction
The Scroll

Nonfiction
Apocalypse: The Coming Judgment of the Nations
Armageddon: Appointment with Destiny
Countdown to the Apocalypse
Creation: Remarkable Evidence of God's Design
Final Warning
Finding Financial Freedom
The Global-Warming Deception
The Handwriting of God
Heaven: The Mystery of Angels
Jesus: The Great Debate
Journey into Eternity
Messiah: War in the Middle East and the Road to Armageddon
The New Temple and the Second Coming
The Next World War
Prince of Darkness
Shadow Government
The Signature of God
Surveillance Society
Triumphant Return
Unveiling Mysteries of the Bible
War on Terror

How Big-Government Liberals
Are Destroying the America You Love

ONE NATION, UNDER ATTACK

GRANT R. JEFFREY

WATERBROOK
PRESS

One Nation, Under Attack
Published by WaterBrook Press
12265 Oracle Boulevard, Suite 200
Colorado Springs, Colorado 80921

All Scripture quotations are taken from the King James Version.

Italics in Scripture quotations reflect the author's added emphasis.

ISBN 978-0-307-73107-4
ISBN 978-0-307-73109-8 (electronic)

Copyright © 2012 by Grant R. Jeffrey

Cover design by Mark D. Ford

Published in the United States by WaterBrook Multnomah, an imprint of the Crown Publishing Group, a division of Random House Inc., New York.

WaterBrook and its deer colophon are registered trademarks of Random House Inc.

Cataloging-in-Publication Data is on file with the Library of Congress.

Printed in the United States of America
2015

10 9 8 7 6 5 4

Special Sales
Most WaterBrook Multnomah books are available at special quantity discounts when purchased in bulk by corporations, organizations, and special-interest groups. Custom imprinting or excerpting can also be done to fit special needs. For information, please e-mail SpecialMarkets@WaterBrookMultnomah.com or call 1-800-603-7051.

Set thine house in order.

2 KINGS 20:1

◻ ◻ ◻

CONTENTS

PUBLISHER'S NOTE

In the fall of 2011, Grant Jeffrey and I were discussing a number of details pertaining to his next book, which you are now holding in your hands. Grant had decided that the book would touch on the expanding upheaval in the Middle East, in particular the worldwide impact of the Arab Spring. He wanted as well to write about the growing economic crisis facing many of the member nations of the European Union as well as the Great Recession in the United States.

It goes without saying that he would establish clear connections between major earthly crises and the unfolding time line of the last days. As you know, Grant was a leading authority on biblical prophecy, and he could see like few other Christians the ways in which world developments foreshadowed the coming apocalypse.

Several weeks later, Grant had concluded his research and was well into the writing of this book. He let me know that economic issues would be dealt with in greater detail, and he decided to use the term *Economic Armageddon* to capture the gravity of the situation.

Grant sent his manuscript to me in late February. I was close to finishing an early edit when I received word that he had been rushed to a hospital. He did not recover from the illness, at least in this life. Grant passed away on May 11, 2012.

I know that Grant died in the same way he lived, which is reflected in the epigraph to this book: "Set thine house in order" (2 Kings 20:1). The verse is a message from God that was communicated through the prophet Isaiah. Grant wanted the verse to appear early in his book and then to appear again at the end of the final chapter. Now you have the opportunity to benefit from Grant's passion to uncover the signs that point to the return of Jesus Christ.

—Ron R. Lee

Senior Editor, WaterBrook Press

July 2012

IN MEMORIAM

Grant Jeffrey grew up at Frontier Ranch in Arnprior, Ontario, Canada, where his parents ran a Christian summer camp for boys and girls. Grant loved riding horses, fishing, camping, hunting, boating, and other sports. He was adventurous and carefree until the age of seventeen, when an accident marked him for the rest of his life. Grant would compare himself with the woman in the Bible who suffered under many physicians. He spent a lot of time over the next few years undergoing operations and procedures that endeavored to improve his quality of life.

When Grant was fourteen, his father took him to a Bible prophecy conference in Ottawa. God stirred his heart and spirit, and he began to read and study the Bible in a new way. He started to collect books and articles from newspapers and magazines pertaining to world events that could lead to the return of Jesus Christ. His library eventually grew to contain more than seven thousand books.

Grant finished high school at the age of seventeen and was accepted into Philadelphia Bible College that fall. He did not feel called into ministry at that time, but he wanted to receive a deeper understanding of the Scriptures. A lifelong student of the Word of God, he received his PhD in biblical studies in 1999 from Louisiana Baptist University.

I met Grant in December 1975, and we were married on August 13, 1977, in London, Ontario. We have a God-given daughter, Adrienne (Jeffrey) Tigchelaar, and a son-in-law, Scott. Grant and I are Papa and

Nana to their children, Christopher and Ben, who never fail to bring great joy.

In 1984 a friend encouraged Grant to write a book on the knowledge God had revealed to him from the Scriptures. In 1988 we set up our own publishing company, Frontier Research Publications, and published Grant's first book, *Armageddon: Appointment with Destiny.* The book hit the market and seemed to explode. Overnight, Grant became an international speaker and a leading teacher on Bible prophecy and the intelligent defense of our Christian faith. God had called Grant and me into full-time ministry.

Over the course of Grant's writing career, he wrote twenty-eight books (*One Nation, Under Attack* is his twenty-ninth). He won the Christy Award for Futuristic Novel for his book *By Dawn's Early Light,* coauthored with Angela Hunt. His most significant work is the *Jeffrey Prophecy Study Bible,* published by Frontier Research Publications in 2009. It is notable that Grant's legacy also includes a God-given discovery that came to light in the pages of his book *Signature of God.* Had he not researched the advanced medical information found in the Bible, there would not be a product line called Hyssop Health, a God-given formula that possesses and conveys tremendous benefits.

Rooted in his personal faith in God, Grant established himself as a leading teacher on biblical prophecy and as one of the sharpest minds in the study of eschatology. He was held in great esteem by his colleagues. His message impacted millions of lives around the world. His amazing insight and his ability to compile vast amounts of facts and figures and then present a clear, concise, pertinent message were remarkable. As a teacher and speaker, he took his message to hundreds of prophecy conferences and parachurch organizations. He was a powerful force in advancing the premillennial view of Bible prophecy. All who sat under his ministry witnessed firsthand his strong desire to present factual proof that the Bible is the Word of God and all are in need of a personal relationship with God.

We traveled the world together. Israel was where Grant's heart longed to be. Archaeology fascinated us as we explored deep underground, in tunnels that run beneath the Western Wall and the City of David. We explored the Qumran Caves and visited many other archaeological sites. In May 2004, Grant received the State of Israel's Loyal Friends of Israel Award for his deep and abiding moral support for Israel and the Jewish people as well as his efforts in stimulating the interest of Christians in investing in Israeli bonds. Grant said, "I accept this award with humility and friendship for the people of Israel and Jews everywhere. This is an opportunity for Christians who love Israel to express their practical support through their financial investment in rebuilding the nation of Israel as prophesied throughout the Word of God." Grant also was honored by the minister of tourism as an Ambassador of Goodwill to Israel.

Grant had a huge presence in the world of radio and television. His program *Bible Prophecy Revealed* is broadcast twice weekly in more than eighty nations on the Trinity Broadcasting Network.

I always admired Grant for being so tuned in to God. God's presence in his life was so strong that he continually poured into my spirit and anyone who came in contact with him. He always believed that with God nothing is impossible. He prayed and believed that one day he would be healed, if not here, then in his eternal home. God took him home to heaven on May 11, 2012, where he has received his victorious healing. Grant will suffer no more.

I am so thankful for the powerful love we had for each other and for our thirty-five years together. It's not over. We will see each other again in the presence of our loving Savior! I can hardly wait!

—Kaye Jeffrey

◻ ◻ ◻

P.S. To all of Grant's faithful readers, we thank you. It was your support and encouragement that inspired Grant to diligently research and study more deeply in God's Word.

ONE NATION,
UNDER ATTACK

Introduction

There Is Far More at Stake Than Most of Us Realize

The United States of America is unique. In the last five thousand years kingdoms, nations, and empires have risen to power, extending their reach and rule over others. But never has there been the equal of the United States in power and world influence.

America is the only nation that was conceived as a limited republic based on divinely inspired biblical principles. God's revealed truth undergirds the Declaration of Independence and the U.S. Constitution. These documents clearly reflect an intentional recognition of God and His work in the world as well as the necessity of basing laws, liberties, and rights on His revealed moral law.

In various ways, all of this helped to transform the thirteen colonies that broke away from England in 1776 into history's most influential and dominant world empire. By the end of World War II, America was unsurpassed in military might and unequalled in technology, manufacturing, economic vitality, and world leadership. The nation that began with New World immigrants seeking independence from Britain replaced the British Empire by virtue of America's international presence, economic leadership, and military power.

The American Empire has been richly blessed by God from the beginning, but in recent decades America has given in to forces that oppose and deny God's intentions for this great nation. The country that has done more than any other to guarantee personal liberties at home and to defend freedom around the world is seeing its power and influence diminish day by day. The American Empire soon will fall from its position as world leader, and its fall will affect every one of us.

America is being pushed to the brink by economic reversals brought on by decades of unsound economic policy and more recently by an overextended military, a deadlocked Congress, and a federal government that chooses again and again to turn its back on the clear intent and wisdom of the Constitution. In a very short time, the United States will be pushed to the sidelines of world events. The center of power and influence will shift away from the nation that has served since the eighteenth century as the model of democracy and individual freedom.

All of this is taking place just prior to the emergence of the prophesied Antichrist. Satan's representative on earth will consolidate his power and first establish his dictatorship over the revived Roman Empire and then over the entire world. The American Empire that rose to power with the blessing of God will be so weak it won't play a notable role in the culminating events of the last days.

This is the greatest of ironies. The only nation in history that was

2

intentionally founded as a limited republic based on God's principles will be powerless to oppose the coming global tyranny of evil.

The Rise and Decline of the American Empire

America's leaders from the start honored God and looked to God's Scriptures for guidance. The colonies won their independence from England in 1783, adopted a constitution, and enjoyed steady growth in political, economic, and military power. By the early twentieth century the United States was coming to the aid of democratic allies around the world and winning the First World War. Then, in World War II, America accepted the responsibility to defend freedom by waging war in Europe, North Africa, Asia, and the South Pacific. At the end of the Second World War, America was the unquestioned, unrivaled leader of the free world. No other world power was positioned to block the threatened expansion of Soviet Russia and Communist China during the Cold War.

In fact, the United States of America was far more than a powerful nation. It was rising to the status of a world empire. Empires expand gradually as they amass power, extend their reach, and assert their influence over the rest of the world.

A commentator on global politics, Harvard professor Michael Ignatieff, wrote about the identifying characteristics of the American Empire. "Ever since George Washington warned his countrymen against foreign entanglements, empire abroad has been seen as the republic's permanent temptation and its potential nemesis. Yet what word but 'empire' describes the awesome thing that America is becoming? It is the only nation that polices the world through five global military commands; maintains more than a million men and women at arms on four continents; deploys carrier battle groups on watch in every ocean; guarantees the survival of countries from Israel to South Korea; drives the wheels of global trade and commerce; and fills the hearts and minds of an entire planet with its dreams and desires."[1]

Like all great empires, America could not hold the course and preserve the things that made it great. A gradual decline began before the end of the 1950s. In recent years external forces orchestrated a coordinated attack that has hastened the empire's decline. Soon the American Empire will fall, and the collapse will come rapidly.

Why Is America Absent from Biblical Prophecy?

The United States is not mentioned specifically in biblical prophecy. It does not appear by name or by geographical reference in the detailed descriptions of events that will occur during the last-days generation. Jesus Christ will return at the Battle of Armageddon to destroy the Antichrist and establish His eternal kingdom on earth.

But the one nation in the West that has benefitted from God's blessing is absent from the prophetic accounts of the critical last-days events.[2]

There is a strange silence regarding the political and military presence and strategic influence of the United States leading up to the two major prophesied wars. In accounts of the War of Gog and Magog (see Ezekiel 38–39), when Russia and its Islamic allies will attempt to invade Israel and annihilate its Jewish population, there is no mention of America's involvement. Ezekiel tells us that the Lord will intervene to supernaturally destroy the millions of invading Russian and Islamic soldiers. He will use earthquakes, fire and brimstone, plagues, and even madness to defeat the invading armies to save His chosen people from genocide. Where in all this is America, the declared ally of Israel?

The Bible's prophecies are equally silent regarding the role of America in the cataclysmic Battle of Armageddon at the end of the seven-year dictatorship of the Antichrist. The prophetic Scriptures provide significant details regarding virtually all the Eastern and Western nations and their military alliances as they relate to this final war on earth. Since every nation on earth will be involved at the Battle of Armageddon, it is certain that America will be present in some fashion, but the lack of a specific mention of America as a key player indicates that the United States will no longer be a leading power in the world.

How can this be? The United States invests more in its military defense than the next ten top nations combined. America dominates the world with more power than any previous empire, including ancient Rome and the British Empire at the height of its supremacy. What can explain the lack of any prophetic reference to the American Empire? What combination of forces will be capable of draining America's power in only a few short years?

A study of history shows that world empires often were defeated by military conquest, but they also are vulnerable to internal forces. For example, while the British Empire found itself on the winning side of World War II, within weeks British citizens voted Prime Minister Winston Churchill out of power. They elected a liberal Labor government that created an enormously expensive and unsustainable welfare state. Wealth was drained from the private sector, and the governing Labor Party virtually disarmed the British military. Within three years the ruling regime dismantled the British Empire that had reigned over almost one-quarter of the globe for more than a century. The left-wing Labor Party abandoned the empire by withdrawing from the Commonwealth nations; Northern Ireland was the lone exception. It took only three years for the socialist Labor Party to destroy the legendary British Empire.

One Nation, Under Attack

The American Empire that saw its birth in the world's first experiment in limited representative government has been undermined by international financiers working together with powerful socialist forces both inside America and overseas. These enemies of free-market capitalism are prepared to launch the final stage of a multipronged attack against America.

Already they have succeeded almost beyond belief in weakening the U.S. economy. For evidence that their strategies are working you need look no further than any newspaper or television news program. They will not stop until they have crippled the national economy, transforming the once-great United States into an impoverished nation with a severely weakened military and no influence on the world stage. A powerless America serves their purposes because it will not be able to resist the movement—being led from within the European Union—that seeks to achieve global governance.

The developments we will examine in the chapters that follow are deliberate and carefully planned. International financiers and other global interests have recruited hundreds of willing accomplices who occupy the most powerful positions in the federal government as well as officials of the European Union who are more than happy to do the bidding of globalist multibillionaires.

No longer will there be a freedom-defending global superpower that works for human rights and fights against the military aggression of other nations. There will no longer be a world power that is committed to advancing free enterprise and the prosperity that comes as a result of free-market capitalism.

One Nation, Under Attack will reveal the blunt truth, and much of it will be difficult to accept. If you love your country, you may not want to believe that your nation's leaders are selling America to the highest bidder. But it is far better to know the truth than be deceived by the Washington propaganda machine.

You need to understand what is taking place so you can protect your family's financial future and safeguard your assets and your property. You need to act now so you will be positioned to withstand the coming collapse of the American Empire. The United States will fall into a state of near oblivion, becoming little more than a helpless bystander, while the most dramatic events in history unfold in Europe, the Middle East, and beyond.

The Antichrist soon will rise to power and enslave the nations of the revived Roman Empire. Initially, he will rule the member nations of the European Union (EU) as well as a number of Mediterranean nations. Once the Antichrist has consolidated his power over this confederation, he will gain control of the entire world.

At a time in history when the political influence, economic power, and military force of the United States could be called into service to oppose this unprecedented spread of evil in the world, America will be sliding into obscurity. The fall of the American Empire is already at an advanced stage. In fact, the end of America's story will come in your lifetime.

1

Now Is the Time to Prepare for America's Fall

Things Have Gone Too Far to Reverse the Slide

S tudents of biblical prophecy understand there is a close connection between what the Hebrew prophets foretold more than twenty-five hundred years ago and what is unfolding in our world today. But often the events are thought to be limited to regions within Europe, Asia, the Middle East, and parts of Africa. In other words, the effects of the fulfillment of prophecy are too often seen as distant, not only in time, but also in geography.

But the developments we are following are right here at home. The analysis I set forth in this book is not mere speculation or the product of an overactive imagination. It comes straight out of the writings of the prophets as well as the headlines of world news and national events.

Here are a few current developments that point to the coming collapse of the American Empire:

- *The work of overseas financiers, in league with federal officials, to manipulate the U.S. economy in ways that are beneficial to overseas interests but soon will bring about the demise of the American Empire.* Those in the top tier of personal wealth who have benefitted from international trade and the overflow of a free-market economy are now pulling the strings to destroy our nation.

- *Documented evidence of the rise of totalitarianism in America.* The so-called imperial presidency has been gaining ground through several recent presidential administrations. But never have we seen the equal of President Barack Obama's brazen power grab.

- *The success of the deliberate strategy to undermine free-market capitalism, knowing that a military attack against America would be doomed to failure.* America's enemies have learned how to use one of our greatest strengths against us. Working covertly to subvert long-held American traditions, these forces are using America's liberties to destroy the nation's economic prosperity.

America cannot remain strong if it cannot remain solvent. It is not just military might but also economic strength that makes it possible to extend American influence in the world. Business growth, trade, investment, and opportunity have fueled the economy since the days of colonial America. But the socialist elites who support a global government cannot achieve their goals unless they first put an end to America's prosperity. If they can succeed in this, America will cease to be a dominant power in the world.

When the War of Gog and Magog is waged in the Middle East—the war that will attempt to annihilate the Jews—America will be powerless to help defend Israel. After that battle, the cataclysmic Battle of Armageddon will take place without an American military presence. What will happen between now and the last days to remove the United States from a position of influence and power?

The Steady Success of the Anti-American Agenda

The conspirators working to destabilize the United States operate through unofficial alliances that all stand to gain as a result of the fall of the American Empire. International financiers and other global interests work in partnership with willing accomplices in the United States. The accomplices occupy powerful positions within the federal government and have counterparts who hold high office in many European governments. These individuals are loyal first and foremost to the multibillionaires who recruited them to advance their socialist cause.

European billionaire socialist George Soros is recognized as the king of this insider deal. He and other power brokers bankroll liberal-progressive political candidates and left-leaning policies and objectives. He and his confederates spend staggering amounts of money in their efforts to defeat conservative and (in the United States) Republican candidates in order to block passage of fiscally responsible, freedom-preserving legislation. Soros and many others who share his agenda pull the strings of highly placed puppets in government. In the United States, Soros's secret partners include President Obama and the top three hundred most powerful officials in Washington.

If you think that sounds like extremist rhetoric, think again. You need do nothing more than follow the political coverage of the major national news organizations. I invite you to monitor the reporting of a liberal news outlet such as the *New York Times* or the *Washington Post.* As you read between the lines of their reporting, take a step back and look at the bigger picture. Notice the story that really is being told.

Here are just a few of the developments we can document. These are drawn from the first three years of the Obama administration:

- While proclaiming that an important goal is U.S. energy inde-pendence, the Obama administration has restricted domestic oil exploration and production. A major pipeline project was vetoed and offshore oil drilling was suspended. One reason America has risen to world leadership as an economic power is due to its abundant, reliable sources of energy. By reducing domestic oil production and, as a result, elevating the cost of energy, the socialist elite is advancing on one front in its effort to cripple the U.S. economy.

- Liberals use protecting the environment as a smokescreen to hide their agenda of penalizing business. On the surface, protecting the environment sounds like a well-intentioned policy—until you look closely at the environmentalist agenda. New regulations imposed by the Environmental Protection Agency (EPA), together with additional restrictions originating with various federal, state, and municipal agencies, have slowed U.S. business expansion. Unnecessary requirements regarding carbon emissions, air and water standards, excessive employee

safety rules, and other interferences have forced major corporations and smaller companies to shift their operations from our
shores to branches in China or India, nations with few restrictive regulations. Naturally, the exporting of U.S. manufacturing, production, and employment to third-world nations drains
wealth from the U.S. economy.

- America is mired in a "jobless" recovery. Why did the U.S.
  stock market steadily regain what it lost in the financial crisis
  of 2008 while the rate of unemployment remained largely flat
  and only very slowly began to creep downward in what has
  been labeled as a jobless recovery? Companies can grow their
  profits in the face of higher operating costs and unreasonable
  regulations only by offshoring their operations. By doing
  so, they not only enjoy lower costs but also encounter far
  less interference in their operations. Meanwhile, Americans
  continue to lose jobs. On the other hand, my home country,
  Canada, has not embraced the environmental extremism of
  the "manmade global warming" movement. With a minimum of environmental regulations, Canada has enjoyed
  the strongest job growth and the greatest general economic
  growth of all nations in the G20 group of leading world
  economies.

It is important to recognize that the carefully planned agenda to
weaken America did not begin with the election of President Obama
in 2008. This anti-American political-economic agenda was set in motion decades earlier and has continued during the last several presidential administrations. The agenda has been steadily advanced regardless of
whether the presidential administration was Republican or Democratic.

Geopolitical Upheaval, Especially in the Muslim World

Seemingly unrelated developments in separate regions of the world often combine to achieve one goal. Diverse strands that appear to operate independently can have the effect of accomplishing a common agenda.

The primary point of attack against the American Empire is the U.S. economy, but everything else flows from that. For instance, it is not widely reported that the Great Recession of 2008 and the slow economic recovery since then have forced U.S. military cutbacks of more than 25 percent. This is a shocking reduction, and it has taken place since President Obama's election. America's role as defender of political freedom around the world is being eroded.

Here are some of the most evident and far-reaching efforts to dismantle the American Empire by destroying its economy.

Continued radical Islamist attacks against Israel and the West

The killing of Osama Bin Laden by U.S. Navy SEALs temporarily disrupted Al-Qaida's anti-Western campaign, but many other Islamic extremist organizations—such as Hamas in Gaza and Hezbollah in Lebanon—are filling the power vacuum. They will renew their attacks on Israel, Europe, and the United States. It also is believed that the death of bin Laden might lead Al-Qaida to become more decentralized, with leaders rising to prominence in different regions.

Power shifts in the Muslim world

The populist revolutions known collectively as the Arab Spring unseated longtime rulers in a number of Muslim nations. While the timing might seem coincidental, the total effect of such uprisings in so many Islamic nations is still playing out. As this book went to press, the Egyptian military had publicly vowed to prevent the newly elected Muslim Brotherhood government from ruling the nation. Meanwhile, the International Committee of the Red Cross declared the prolonged armed violence in Syria to be a full-scale civil war. On a broader scale, analysts continue to study regime changes in North Africa and the Middle East in an attempt to predict whether new national leaders will be more strongly anti-Western than their predecessors.

It is known that the toppling of so-called moderate, pro-Western regimes in many Arab nations means that a more radicalized, anti-Western Islamic leadership is likely to assume power. If that comes to pass, more nations than ever before will be ruled by the legal strictures of shari'ah law.

In a related development, regime changes in oil-producing nations also raise the specter of disruptions in petroleum supplies. As Americans saw with the rise in gasoline prices after the United Nations imposed sanctions on Iran in 2012, shifts in policy or leadership create an inevitable disruption of energy supplies. Increased energy prices in the West are a further impediment to economic recovery.

Potential interruption of ocean trade routes

With the ongoing political instability in Egypt there remains the possibility of a closing of the Suez Canal, or barring that, restrictions on movement through the canal. Such a move by Egypt's leadership (the nature of that leadership is still in dispute as of this writing) would disrupt the global transportation of goods and raw materials. A radicalized Egyptian regime might choose to limit Western (or Israeli) access to the canal.

God's Prophets Foresaw These Developments

It's important to piece together the seemingly unrelated geopolitical and economic developments in the world. At the same time, we can make sense of these developments only when we view them in light of biblical prophecy. What do the ancient Hebrew prophets tell us about the meaning of recent power shifts in the Arab world as well as in the wider Muslim world?

For one, the focus on the Arab Spring shows us that the center of power has shifted away from the West (including America). The center of power now is concentrated in regions of the world that possess energy resources amid radicalized politics that are linked closely to religion. The energy-producing nations always have possessed a high degree of power and influence, but only recently, with the overthrow of somewhat pro-Western regimes, has the West faced the serious threat of anti-American centers of power using petroleum as a weapon.

A curtailment of oil shipments would have an immediate and catastrophic impact. Even if oil shipments continued at current levels, these regimes are likely to use petrodollars from the West to finance intensified acts of terrorism against the West.

As a student of prophecy and world events for decades, I am confident in saying we should prepare for a series of unprecedented political, economic, and military crises. These will feed on one another, heightening the impact of the combined shifts in policy, priorities, and freedoms. Humanity will be buffeted by a series of escalating crises, beginning with the American financial and monetary weakness that continues more than four years after the nation's initial economic meltdown.

Economic weakness leads to political instability and a steep decline in a nation's military capabilities. So it is only logical that the solution begins with restoring America's economic strength. The socialist elite, however, has rigged the system to ensure that we will never recover our former economic health and stability.

A nation cannot maintain its economic strength on borrowed money, and America is the world's largest borrower. In contrast, only four decades ago the United States was the world's largest creditor nation. As anyone knows who has tried to invigorate a family budget by overspending with credit cards, financial health can never be achieved through debt. It is just the opposite—debt eats away at financial confidence and erodes growth.

In later chapters we will expose the economic attacks on America, but that is just one of many fronts where the American Empire is under attack. The power shifts in the Middle East are significant, as is the loss of moral fortitude to defend freedom and representative democracy at home. We will detail the progress of the globalist-socialist strategies now moving forward to bleed America dry financially, even as these forces succeed in limiting and denying our constitutional liberties.

As a lead-up to the final global Battle of Armageddon, certain conditions will come about. We can read these conditions as signs of what is soon to take place. This is another reason why it is essential that we follow today's news with a critical eye. To finance the two-hundred-million-man army of the East that will invade Israel, the invading nations will need to amass wealth, armaments, military personnel, and more.

With that in mind, we can identify several world developments that point to preparations for the last days.

- Energy-producing nations will continue to amass wealth while energy-consuming nations will continue to decline. Along with the imbalance in energy production, energy-consuming nations will lose their bargaining power as well as their national autonomy and freedom to OPEC and other commodities suppliers such as China and Russia.

- The deepening financial crises in the euro zone should open our eyes to the global nature of the economic catastrophe that looms in the near future. European banks continue to exhibit signs of weakness, and the European Union is divided on how and how much to assist member nations whose economies are insolvent.

- Consider the long-term effects of years of uncontrolled illegal immigration into the United States. Not only do illegal immigrants shut off U.S. citizens from employment opportunities, the immigrants have reintroduced many infectious, often fatal diseases that were thought to have been eradicated years ago.

- Punitive and misguided federal energy policies will sabotage America's energy future for generations. Washington DC has raised false hopes by linking the nation's "energy independence" to ineffective wind power, solar power, and geothermal power, draining enormous wealth and resources from the U.S. economy. Meanwhile, exploration for new sources of petroleum and drilling are tightly restricted.

All these developments, plus many others not listed here, are enough to send the United States into an economic nosedive that will exceed the damage of the Great Depression. No longer will the United States exercise a dominant global influence. No longer will any free nation be able to count on America to come to its aid. Aggressor nations will no longer fear the threat of U.S. intervention and retaliation because, very soon, America will be too weak to take action anywhere.

Meanwhile, it is crucial to recognize the power as well as the person that is staged to fill the power vacuum by introducing a global dictatorship. The Antichrist is alive today somewhere in Europe or the Middle East. He is being groomed to step into his global leadership role at this moment. The way is being paved for his elevation to power by the same international globalist conspirators who are pulling down America.

Who are these conspirators (the puppets and the leaders who are pulling their strings)? To answer that question, think first about who will benefit most from the bankrupting of America and in what ways they will benefit. Why would multibillionaires support totalitarianism and socialist economic policies, which historically are the enemies of entrepreneurship, investment, private property, and free enterprise?

The best evidence reveals they do not back wealth creation for any but themselves, and they are most interested in exploiting America's wealth for their own profit and political advantage. They support capitalism only when they can manipulate the system for their own purposes and profit.

Most of the billionaire socialists who support globalism are dedicated to reducing America's prosperity as well as its role as the leader of the free world. America's continued weakness will only work in their favor.

In the chapters that follow I will point out what is happening right now. But once the facts are revealed, other people have to act. Analysts alone cannot reverse the decline and fall of a world empire. The challenge is the same for all writers who uncover the hidden dangers of the cultural, military, economic, and social collapse taking place in America.

Most of these developments have been evident since the 1950s, but they are easy to overlook if you're not constantly aware of the threat. Things could have gone over the cliff in the 1980s, triggered by the recession of that decade. However, there was plenty of forward momentum in the nation's economy. With such a large economy, momentum can last for decades.

Helping to sustain America's economy were the productivity boom and the collapse of the Soviet Union in 1991. Further, China unexpectedly liberalized its economic policies, and communism was discredited around the world (except in Cuba, North Korea, and on many U.S. college campuses). The end of the Cold War opened up vast areas of the world to the global market. Most surprising, Federal Reserve chairman Paul Volker tightened the money supply, forcing interest rates to rise, thus motivating Americans to save money and stop excessive borrowing.

But unsustainable government polices eventually caught up to and exceeded the ability of American businesses to absorb and overcome the damage. Since 2008 and growing more dangerous year by year, the borrowing and monetary expansion decisions of the Obama administration and the Federal Reserve have reached the inevitable result. As detailed in the following chapters, we will see that unchecked increases in the federal budget deficit and the national debt, combined with the Federal Reserve's staggering expansion of the money supply, will push the American Empire to the brink of collapse. These two forces working together will produce a devastating level of inflation that will destroy the savings and investments of millions of Americans. The livelihoods of retirees living on fixed incomes will disappear. The life savings of hundreds of millions of Americans will be wiped out. This approaching economic disaster will change your business, your work, your assets and investments, and your life in ways that most people cannot imagine.

The problems caused by the multipronged attack on the American economy go far beyond political campaigns or partisan squabbles in the Congress. The fallout from this will affect every household in America.

If you know in advance what is about to happen, you will have the advantage of taking early action to protect your assets and secure a financial future for your family. It is too late for the economy to be saved, but it is not too late for you to take the necessary steps to protect your wealth from the worst of what will devastate other families. Yet there is nothing you or any politician can do to prevent the approaching crisis.

This crisis will dramatically affect your savings, your investments, and your plans for retirement. This debt-fueled inflationary crisis will change virtually everything concerning your way of life: where you vacation, where you send your children or grandchildren to school, and how and where you spend your money.

When prices for commodities such as milk, bread, and gasoline soar at an unprecedented rate, you need to know what to do. When banks begin to close their doors to depositors and when credit cards are no longer accepted for purchases, when ATM machines stop working, when you are not able to get your hands on cash to make purchases and pay bills, what will you do? How will you choose an alternate approach when you are not able to buy gold or exchange dollars for a more reliable foreign currency? (In chapter 9 we will look at ways you can protect your family and your future.)

You might choose to doubt the accuracy of what I will reveal in the following chapters. Or you might interpret the signs differently. But if you follow my analysis, I believe you will realize that most of the moves against America have already been made. All that is needed is a little more time for the process to have its full, fatal impact.

In chapter 2 we will examine in detail how the enemies of free-market capitalism have succeeded in destroying history's most prosperous, most successful nation.

2

The American Empire's Financial Collapse

The Full-Scale Rush to Economic Armageddon

Years of excessive federal borrowing and spending are leading the United States toward a dark day of reckoning. The financial collapse that is looming will make the 2008 financial meltdown look like a minor course correction. The day of reckoning that lies ahead can be accurately characterized as Economic Armageddon.

Individual citizens are starting to sense that the American Dream of increased prosperity and rising standards of living from one generation to the next are turning into a nightmare. Economists use a percentage figure to compare the relative standards of living of nations throughout the world. The percentage reveals the value of the country's annual production (gross domestic product, or GDP) divided by the population. This measure provides a reasonable benchmark to compare national economies. The measure also illustrates the growth or decline in wealth within a nation over time, which most economists view as a fundamental and fair measure of a country's economic success or failure.

Of course we are interested in the measure of America's economic success or failure. However, bear in mind that the government's nominal GDP figures are greatly distorted by continuing inflation. Inflation, which inevitably reduces our standard of living, ironically drives *up* the government's estimates of the GDP. As a result, factoring inflation into the calculation creates the false appearance of a wealthier country while the reality is that the average American family is getting poorer.

Consider sales of new automobiles, which reached a peak in 1985 with 11 million vehicles sold. This statistic has been declining at a steady rate since 1999. By 2009, Americans bought only 5.4 million new passenger cars, a reduction of 51 percent in twenty-four years, and this happened in spite of a growing population. As a consequence, the median age of a registered vehicle in the United States is now almost ten years.

The average college student upon graduation has accumulated an average of $24,000 in tuition debt. Before young adults reach age thirty, they owe an average of more than $6,000 in credit card debt. When we consider the median annual earnings for Americans aged twenty-five to thirty-four, which ranges from $34,000 to $38,000, we see that young adults begin their productive income years with a debt-to-income ratio of nearly one to one.[1]

Meanwhile, when we look at households headed by people older than sixty-two, we find that debt levels have been rising since 1991. A study by William Apgar of Harvard's Joint Center for Housing Studies found that the average mortgage among this group is $71,000, which is five times larger than the same measure in 1987, when adjusted for inflation.[2]

USA Today reported that lower- and middle-income Americans aged sixty-five and older owe an average of more than $10,000 in credit card debt, up 26 percent since 2005. In light of average interest rates of 20 percent for credit card debt, it is unlikely that these debts will ever be fully repaid.

The national debt problem combined with continuing inflation and the devaluation of the dollar will force the government to raise interest rates. Such a move will be an attempt to suppress rising rates of inflation, but it will bring other unwanted consequences. A rise in interest rates will slow business expansion and job creation. Companies will have to absorb the cost of higher interest on business loans while consumers and homeowners will suffer by paying significantly higher interest costs when existing low rates on a variable interest mortgage will be renewed at higher and often unaffordable rates.

The Federal Reserve has attempted to create the illusion of a monetary and economic recovery through a policy of maintaining interest rates at historic lows (almost zero percent!). Meanwhile, the Fed has relentlessly used its printing presses to monetize its debt while enlarging the U.S. money supply by an unthinkable 300 percent between 2008 and 2010. This was a vain attempt to delay the inevitable day when America will be forced to live within its means. That day is coming, and none of us can picture all the things that will mean.

Financial Abuses That Eventually Wreak Havoc

Highly leveraged investment contracts known as derivatives were a major cause of the real estate and debt-crisis meltdowns that came dangerously close in 2008 to wiping out most of America's biggest banks. Beyond that, these high-risk investments came frighteningly close to destroying the entire U.S. economy. It was a closer call than the federal government wanted to admit, but in spite of that, financial institutions have refused to abandon their terribly risky derivative contracts and other high-risk investment practices.

American banks held $176 *trillion* in derivatives at the height of the global debt crisis in 2008. By 2012, U.S. banks had *increased* these high-risk investments to $244 trillion—nearly 40 percent higher than the 2008 level (according to the office of the Comptroller of the Currency, a division of the U.S. Treasury Department). As a consequence of this financial exposure, the United States is in *far greater* economic danger than many other countries. The world's most successful investor, Warren Buffett, described the dangerous practices of U.S. banks and investment houses as "financial weapons of mass destruction."[3]

These financial excesses have not simply continued, they have been multiplied. An Economic Armageddon appears to be unavoidable. Already we can see that irresponsible fiscal policies and practices by major banks as well as the federal government are stealing wealth from the American people through inflation. The explanation for why the federal government refuses to acknowledge this growing inflation in America can be found in a quote from 147 years ago. As the French poet and essayist Charles Baudelaire wrote in "The Generous Gambler," "The loveliest trick of the Devil is to persuade you that he does not exist!"[4]

For nearly twelve years we have seen multiple billions of dollars in deficit spending, begun during the administration of George W. Bush and continued under President Obama. America has added a staggering amount of new debt just since the 2008 election. While President Obama promised hope and change, he has continued the old habit of federal waste and overspending. Instead of working to match spending to revenues, the federal government borrows more and more money. The U.S. Treasury creates trillions of dollars out of thin air by printing more currency. While new money appears to a casual observer to cost virtually nothing, the reality is that the Federal Reserve devalues personal wealth every time it pumps more currency into circulation.

Few voters anticipated that the Democrat-dominated Congress and President Obama would throw *all* financial caution to the wind during the first two years of his administration. Yet the Obama administration initiated an unprecedented expansion of the money supply, far exceeding the rate of growth of U.S. productivity. This cannot help but create significant inflation and inevitably the devaluation of the American dollar.

How America Has Guaranteed Its Own Destruction

After severely criticizing the Bush administration for its reckless deficit spending, President Obama embarked upon the most irresponsible expansion of government spending in history. The federal government is guilty of overspending more than $1 trillion every year since 2009, when Obama took office. A warning from the Congressional Budget Office (CBO) states that the cost of servicing the national debt will demand an ever greater share of the federal budget as interest rates rise. The CBO projects that net interest costs linked to the national debt will grow from 1.4 percent of GDP in 2012 to as much as 2.5 percent in 2022.[5]

Further, according to the CBO, Obama's 2012 budget proposal would add $6.4 trillion in deficits over the next decade. This report contradicted the White House claim that its 2012 budget request would reduce deficits by $3.2 trillion during the rest of the decade. (The CBO estimate incorporated Obama's announced plans to significantly reduce the military budget by withdrawing all troops from Afghanistan.[6])

To understand how deficit spending puts America in danger, consider that by 2017 annual interest payments on the national debt will begin to equal and then quickly exceed the amount Washington will be spending on Medicaid, the state-federal healthcare program available to tens of millions of poor and disabled Americans.

The Recent Past Gives Clues to Our Future

By 2008 serious economists and financial commentators could see that the coming economic devastation was unavoidable regardless of any policies Washington might implement. Both the residential real estate market and the stock market collapsed. Homeowners found themselves paying on mortgages that exceeded the declining values of their homes, and they started to walk away from their financial obligation. The credit markets dried up as financial institutions began once again to realistically evaluate the credit worthiness of those who applied for loans. U.S. banks experienced a liquidity meltdown, and consequently unemployment began to rise to levels unseen since the Great Depression.

The true rate of unemployment is far higher than the officially reported 8.2 percent at the time of this writing.[7] The more accurate figure is a far higher 17 to 20 percent. And the average figure during President Obama's first three years in office is an astonishing 16.5 percent! This true rate of unemployment exceeds the highest mark reached during all the presidential administrations since the Great Depression. The previous post-Depression record was set by President Jimmy Carter at 15.2 percent, and federal debt under Carter (a Democrat) hit $907 billion. Today, after years of unrestrained spending under a series of Republican and Democratic presidents and congresses, the national debt is just short of $16 trillion. And there is no end in sight.

How do citizens benefit from such extreme spending? Between 2008 and 2012, only the handful of Americans who received money through bailouts and stimulus programs, which could reach $23.7 trillion when all is said and done, could be said to have benefitted.[8]

How Much Is $23.7 Trillion?

When economic analysts discuss federal spending, they speak rather casually in terms of millions, billions, and trillions of dollars. It is difficult for ordinary Americans, who are concerned about the cost of groceries or a gallon of gasoline, to fathom what a billion or a trillion amounts to. Here is one way to picture the cost of the federal bailouts and stimulus programs. According to Representative Darrell Issa (R-CA), "If you spent a million dollars a day going back to the birth of Christ, that wouldn't even come close to just one trillion dollars. $23.7 trillion is a staggering figure." Issa is the chairman of the House Committee on Oversight and Government Reform.

To help understand what lies ahead for America, we will look at conditions in this country during the Great Depression of the 1930s.

Beginning with the stock market crash of 1929, a massive wave of home foreclosures and personal and corporate bankruptcies undercut the nation's financial stability. During the next three years, wages and consumer prices fell by approximately a third. As businesses found they could no longer afford to pay their employees, employees understandably could no longer pay their bills. The snowball effect of economic upheaval spread and threatened every sector of the economy.

The 2008 recession has been called the Great Recession. Soon, the repeated flawed decisions and failed policies of recent years will do their work and bring us to the threshold of Economic Armageddon. As the national debt soars, a number of factors are coming together to move us beyond a point of no return. It is helpful to have a working understanding of the leading causes so that individuals and families can avoid the worst of the harm soon to be inflicted on America.

The U.S. Housing Credit Bubble

The bursting of the housing credit bubble in 2008 was just one symptom of a failed financial system that for years had trusted in the unsustainable basis of debt. The mirage of prosperous United States and European Union financial systems evaporated, and the instability of a global economy based on debt was exposed. In a healthy capitalist economy, this severe downturn would trigger a painful readjustment. During the transition back to stability, people would be exposed to widespread hardships, but eventually the experience would serve as a needed corrective to restore financial vitality.

Yet in an economy already weakened by too many consecutive years of deficit spending, the bursting of the housing credit bubble could not simply be absorbed by the U.S. economy. Instead, it led to a meltdown. U.S. housing prices experienced extraordinary growth from 1997 to 2007 due to relaxed regulations and a dismantling of the rules governing loan ratios and enforcing conservative financial standards. In the past, financial institutions were required to determine the creditworthiness of a mortgage applicant before approving a loan. A Democrat majority in Congress, however, initiated the relaxation of mortgage-issuing standards. The stated intent was to increase the number of families that could qualify for mortgages. The result, though, was these laws made it far too easy for financially strapped families to believe they could afford higher mortgage debt than was manageable at their income level.

The legislation created a mortgage category privately known as ninja loans (no income, no job, no assets). By increasing the pool of home-buyers (though many were unable to manage their mortgage payments), the demand for homes rose significantly. First-time home purchasers and others who took advantage of easily obtained mortgages, beginning in 2002, pushed the housing market to new heights.

Rising home prices due to increased demand, however, were an il-lusion. As growing numbers of homebuyers borrowed more than they could afford and then defaulted on their mortgages, the bubble started to burst. To compound the problem, financial institutions repackaged these unsafe "garbage loans" into toxic investments through securitiza-tion. They sold these combined mortgages to clients who did not fathom the dangers of these investments.

Between 1980 and 2001 U.S. home prices increased at a typical, expected rate similar to the rate of inflation. But the change in mortgage lending rules in 2001 facilitated years of quickly rising housing prices. Home prices rose, but this was not matched by an increase in annual incomes and productivity. The housing bubble was based on an illusion, and the only possible outcome was a major disaster. Standard & Poor's Case-Shiller index is the real estate industry's most trusted source of residential price information. A 2011 Case-Shiller report revealed that the median price of a home in the United States had dropped more than *31 percent* and was continuing to fall.[9]

The bursting of the housing bubble triggered a chain reaction of economic crashes, including a plunge in stock prices, a tightening of credit for businesses and individuals, and reduced consumer spending.

Failing to Learn from Past Mistakes

Even in light of the reversals of previous years, President Obama increased the national debt to unprecedented levels through $1.5 trillion deficits each year in 2009, 2010, and 2011. This produced two additional bubbles: a devaluation of the dollar and a doubling of the national debt in only two years. Let's put this into context. For 232 years, dating back to 1776, the cumulative national debt amounted to $8 trillion. That is the total debt over almost two and a half centuries. Incredibly, the Obama administration managed to nearly double that amount in just two years!

The official national debt was reported to be $15.6 trillion in 2010, but that number merely tells us what the government defines as the amount the nation owes. The more revealing numbers come to the fore when we take into account the unfunded liabilities and entitlement programs bankrolled by the federal government. With those in view, the government's total indebtedness is closer to $100 trillion. This is a hole so deep that the actual debt can never be repaid.[10]

The same type of financial disaster will soon descend on state capitals from coast to coast. State liabilities for unfunded or partially funded pension programs and retiree healthcare benefits already far exceed the likelihood of state governments to provide the necessary funding. When state retiree healthcare benefits are included, the total unfunded liabilities of state governments exceed $1 trillion.[11] These massive debts, while legally binding and as real as your utilities bill, are not carried on the books of any state budget. The promise of pension benefits made to retired state employees, for instance, among other long-term liabilities, add up to a bill that state governments cannot possibly pay.

A much larger financial liability is owed by the federal government. The lion's share of the national debt can be traced to government commitments to pay future benefits to veterans and retired federal employees, together with tens of trillions of dollars committed to Social Security and Medicare. These financial commitments are easily overlooked because the federal government operates on a cash basis. The budget is concerned only with income and expenses between two points in time: from October 1 in one year to September 30 in the following year. Therefore, commitments to pay trillions of dollars in future benefits generally do not show up as financial obligations.

It is difficult to pin down reliable figures that tell the full story. The difficulties are due, in part, to the vast size of the numbers involved. But beyond that, the sources for economic statistics—especially when making future projections—often are biased by political agendas. Finally, definitions vary in terms of what is included in statistics that define, for instance, the true rate of unemployment or the government's future indebtedness. However, it is worth making a careful attempt to determine the scale of the problem.

The federal debt—calculated as the cumulative value of all past budget deficits less surpluses—was $10.2 trillion on September 30, 2011. But the federal government is also committed to paying $5.8 trillion in the future to federal employees and veterans. Social Security's unfunded liability, including the promised benefits in excess of expected Social Security revenues, amounts to another $9.2 trillion during the next seventy-five years. Medicare's unfunded liability is $24.6 trillion.

To understand the devastating financial situation America is in, we must consider the following: after the inauguration of President Obama in January 2009, his budget ran a deficit of $1.4 trillion in the first year. U.S. tax revenues for 2010 totaled $2.162 trillion, but federal expenditures were $3.456 trillion. This created another deficit of $1.3 trillion. In 2011, for the third year in a row, the Obama administration produced a deficit of $1.5 trillion.

The total national debt rose to $14.825 trillion while the GDP in 2011 was $14.66 trillion. Therefore, America's debt-to-GDP ratio is an unhealthy 101.1 percent. At the present rate of rapidly rising government expenditures and exploding annual deficits, the United States is on track to reach an unsustainable national debt to GDP that will exceed 150 percent by 2020 or sooner.[12]

For a revealing comparison, consider that much of the world's attention has been focused on the debt problems of many of the nations in the southern region of the euro zone, especially Greece, Spain, Italy, and Portugal. Using a standard measure of economic health based on the percentage of national GDP represented by its national debt, here are the measures for three struggling euro zone nations:

Greece: public debt is 142.7 percent of GDP (2010 estimate)

Italy: public debt is 119.1 percent of GDP (2010 estimate)

Portugal: public debt is 93 percent of GDP (2010 estimate)

The same measure of relative economic health for the United States in 2011 is 101.1 percent. If the United States were part of the euro zone, it would make Portugal look healthy by comparison.[13]

The fundamental economic reality that no nation can escape is this: you cannot save a country that is drowning in debt by taking on more debt. The logic behind that theory is the same as trying to save a drowning man by throwing water at him. Neither a family nor a nation can continually spend more than it earns each year and expect to find financial stability. Centuries ago the famous English philosopher Samuel Johnson summed up the essence of a healthy and balanced financial life: "Whatever you have, spend less."

A huge percentage of America's debt (more than $4 trillion) is represented by U.S. Treasury bills, of which the vast majority were sold to other nations, especially China, Japan, and Taiwan. Despite the staggering amount of borrowing by the federal government, this amount of $4 trillion will not be enough to cover the expenses of the Obama administration.

The Troubled Asset Relief Program (TARP) was an unprecedented $700 billion federal bailout that shored up big banks that the administration believed were "too big to fail." TARP money also was used to bail out the domestic auto industry, providing taxpayer money of almost $11,000 for every General Motors and Chrysler vehicle sold through the end of 2010. Although the TARP bailout was unprecedented, this was far from being the only such program introduced by the Bush and Obama administrations.

Taxpayers were subsequently forced to pay for another $500 billion federal takeover of weak banks and then a $430 billion bailout used to extend unemployment insurance, infuse pension funds, and bankroll a cash-for-clunkers program to encourage owners of older cars to replace them with new cars. Congress also decided to rescue the Federal National Mortgage Association (better known as Fannie Mae) and the Federal Home Loan Mortgage Corporation (popularly known as Freddie Mac), the U.S. government agencies responsible for insuring toxic mortgages. Congress authorized the Treasury Department to purchase Fannie Mae and Freddie Mac stock for up to $400 billion.

How the Federal Reserve Attacks Your Personal Wealth

The Obama administration's appetite for spending nonexistent dollars has led the federal government to print more money, creating trillions of dollars out of nothing. Between 2008 and 2011, the Federal Reserve created a staggering $1.6 trillion in new currency. Much of this was to finance the $700 billion Troubled Asset Relief Program as well as hundreds of billions of dollars needed to cover additional federal stimulus programs. The long-term effect of printing more money—which is hardly ever acknowledged by the government—is that it fuels inflation.

While the government declares that the official rate of inflation is less than 3 percent, most independent economists believe the true inflation rate exceeds 11 percent. For example, the purchasing power of $20 in 1970 would now require $116 in hard-earned cash. If we were to go back to 1913 (the year the Federal Reserve System was created), $20 in that year's purchasing power would require $457 today.

Even though the White House claims inflation is around 3 percent, every private citizen can see higher prices at the grocery store and gas stations. In 2011 the price of butter jumped 22 percent, gasoline prices soared 35 percent, and coffee rose 42 percent. In general, food prices rose

57 percent during the first two years of the Obama administration. Gas prices were up 34 percent in 2009 and 2010 while cotton prices, an essential clothing commodity, stood at its highest prices in 150 years, rising 210 percent since Obama's inauguration.

During the first two years of the Obama administration, the president and Federal Reserve chairman Ben Bernanke waged a hidden inflation war on the middle class. If you are part of the broad swath of middle-income citizens, your real wealth was reduced by a greater amount in two years than it had been during the previous twenty years. The Federal Reserve under Bernanke and his predecessor, Alan Greenspan, redefined the official rate of inflation numerous times, which enabled them to hide dangerous increases in the prices of food, energy, and other critical, everyday items. Nevertheless, American consumers can see the truth behind every lie every time they pay their bills.

Inflation Is Your Enemy

Throughout most of history, the value of money has been closely tied to tangible, high-value commodities such as gold or silver. Still, President Richard Nixon in 1971 broke the connection between the U.S. dollar and the price of gold. Now, virtually every money system in the world is a fiat currency, based on nothing but the full faith and promise of the issuing nation. As a result, every government is free to increase or decrease its supply of money through its central bank.

The Federal Reserve has been increasing the money supply in amounts that far exceed what is warranted by America's economic growth. As GDP rises, the Federal Reserve must increase the money supply by an equal amount to maintain a healthy economy. However, when the central bank increases the money supply at a faster rate than GDP, inflation results. Because it takes between two and three years for an increased money supply to work its way through the economy, many people and most politicians do not understand that inflation is inevitable whenever the increase in money supply exceeds the rate of the GDP.

There are three ways a government can raise the money it needs for expenses. The first is to raise taxes. However, raising taxes causes the government to lose voter support. Remember, the number-one job of a politician is to get reelected. Therefore raising taxes is avoided as long as possible. The second method is to borrow from the public through government bonds and Treasury bills, but that is also not very attractive to citizens or, consequently, to politicians. The third method is for the Federal Reserve to increase the money supply. Naturally, for the president and Congress, the third option is the most attractive because it appears to be a pain-free option.

While many in government and the news media blame union wage demands, greedy businessmen, overspending by consumers, severe weather, and rising energy prices for inflation, those are not the causes of inflation. While these factors can cause certain prices to rise, only the government's excessive expansion of the money supply can produce general inflation throughout the economy. As the late respected economist and presidential advisor Milton Friedman noted, "Inflation is always and everywhere a monetary phenomenon in the sense that it is and can be produced only by a more rapid increase in the quantity of money than in output."[14]

America will be confronted with untenable inflation within two years due to the astonishing increase in the money supply. How bad can things get? In the 1920s, Germany's Weimar Republic faced economic ruin due to the ruinous demands for war reparations after Germany's loss in World War I. Since war reparations were denominated in German marks, the Weimar government responded by ordering a staggering increase in the money supply. The Western allies received the prescribed reparations, but due to hyperinflation, the value of these payments was almost nothing. Hyperinflation devalued the German currency at an average rate of 300 percent per month for more than a year in 1923 and 1924. German marks were exchangeable for U.S. dollars in 1914 with an exchange rate of approximately four marks per dollar. After the massive increase in the German monetary supply, by 1923 the exchange rate approached *one trillion* marks per dollar. Workers had to be paid several times daily and allowed to leave their jobs to buy basic essentials, because if they waited until the end of the day, the wages they earned in the morning would be worth almost nothing.

Give that some serious thought. It is time for us all to start protecting ourselves against Economic Armageddon.

Why the Government Lies to You About the Economy

Here Is the Truth Behind the Falsified "Official" Statistics

A s the United States rushes toward Economic Armageddon, the federal government is doing its best to keep you from learning the truth. The facts about the weakening national economy are sobering even if you are willing to accept at face value the official reports out of Washington. But when you look at the true story of what is happening—beyond the manipulated statistics the government releases—you will see clearly what is in store for every citizen beginning in the next twenty-four months.

As a tool to use in understanding the devastating developments to come, this chapter compiles statistics and economic reports that the government fails to make available. After you read this analysis of the unemployment rate, the effects of rising inflation, and the certainty of much higher interest rates, you will have a more complete and more sobering picture of where America is headed.

The Sustained Attack on the Middle Class

When you adjust for inflation, the median wage of American males has dropped by 27 percent over the last four decades. In the four years following 2007 the median household income, when adjusted for inflation, declined by 6.8 percent. Real wages for workers continued to fall after three years of President Obama's promised hope and change. The number of Americans living in poverty (49.1 million) was at its highest level in fifty-one years. This number represents one out of every seven families in America trying to survive with a household income amounting to less than $21,954.

The Bureau of Labor Statistics reported that the true average hourly earnings of American workers (based on purchasing power) fell 1.1 percent between February 2011 and February 2012. The truth is that Americans are being squeezed economically far more than the Bureau of Labor Statistics figures indicate. One indication of this is the April 2012 report of the Department of Agriculture that more than 46.4 million Americans were using some form of food stamps—the highest number in history.

Meanwhile, the cost of standard goods and services is rising much faster than the government indicates in its reports. Officially, the consumer price index rose only 2.9 percent in 2011, but these calculations deliberately excluded dramatic increases in the prices of gasoline and food. The American Institute for Economic Research helps put this in perspective. It compiles an Everyday Price Index, which includes the cost of items that consumers buy at least monthly. The Everyday Price Index rose 7.2 percent in 2011, more than double the official consumer price index.

Hiding the Truth About Unemployment

More than 25 million Americans were unemployed or underemployed in 2012, a figure that approached the economic pain of the Great Depression. A tragic measure of the depth of the economic crisis is that after a person loses a job, it takes an average of twenty-five weeks—almost half a year—to find a new one. According to the Bureau of Labor Statistics, in June 2012 unemployment was at 14.4 percent for African Americans and 11 percent for Hispanics. Unemployment among teenagers stood at nearly 25 percent.

While globalism has produced many economic benefits, millions of Americans are unemployed because jobs are being offshored to other nations. It is tempting for companies to build plants in Asia or Mexico, where wage levels are a fraction of what the American labor market demands. In addition, companies that shift production and hiring to other nations often save even more money by eliminating pensions and health benefits and by avoiding environmental regulations. Alan S. Blinder, an economist at Princeton University, estimates that by the year 2030 up to 29 percent of current U.S. jobs will be lost to business operations being moved overseas. As an example of the changed nature of American employment, consider that during the recession of 2001 some 2 percent of U.S. jobs were lost and not restored for four years.

The government tries to minimize the magnitude of the problem by redefining words in ways that make the crisis seem less severe. For example, most of us are not aware that the federal government reimagined the word *unemployment*. In 1994, federal agencies adopted a new definition. One aspect of the new definition is that people who become discouraged after six months of fruitless searching for employment are dropped from the rolls of those who are seeking employment. These people are still unemployed, but under the terms of the new definition, they are no longer counted among the unemployed.

This statistical sleight of hand allows the government to underreport the unemployment rate, which creates an illusion that the economy is doing better than reality would suggest. According to the Bloomberg financial website, the true rate of unemployment, when underemployment is included, is 17 percent. This figure is more than twice as high as the government's official figure of 8.2 percent (as of June 2012).

There is more. As the overall population increases and more people reach working age, the economy needs to expand to create more jobs for more Americans. The opposite has been happening, yet the Obama administration has issued statistics that deny it. In 2011, the U.S. population rose by 1,726,000 while the number of Americans accounted for in the labor force dropped by 67,000. If you look at the government's "not in the labor force" statistics for 2011, you'll see the number rose by 1,793,000. The labor force consists of workers who draw a paycheck, which includes workers drawing unemployment benefits. Workers who lose their job and go on unemployment remain part of the labor force for the purposes of government reporting; however, workers who fail to find a new job by the time their unemployment checks run out are dropped from the labor-force statistic. They are no longer counted as unemployed—whether they are then newly reemployed or remain unemployed.

Why would the federal government pretend that unemployed workers who are not able to find new employment simply disappear from the labor force? Just because workers cannot find jobs does not mean they are no longer interested in working. Here is one reason for subtracting able-bodied but unemployed workers from the labor force statistic: when the population increases while the size of the labor force shrinks, the statistics can create the illusion of an economic recovery.

The true state of affairs, however, is just the opposite. Without this statistical sleight of hand, the accurate numbers show that the unemployment rate increased significantly. An honest accounting shows actual long-term unemployment bordering on 12 percent. Using average labor-force growth statistics from 1948 to 2007, the labor force should have expanded by 6,316,000 since 2007. The actual expansion, though, is less that 40,000, meaning that some 6,276,000 unemployed people are simply unaccounted for in the government's labor statistics.

The Insanity of "Tax the Rich" Plans

Many commentators, including outspoken activists in the Occupy Wall Street movement, claim that those in the top 1 percent of income earners in America are profiting unfairly at the expense of the remaining 99 percent. There is, in fact, a great chasm developing in the distribution of wealth in America. And the disparity is growing wider.

According to a study by economists at the Federal Reserve, "Since 1979, the average income of the top 1 percent has increased 275 percent, while average overall wages are basically unchanged. In the last 10 years, the trend has accelerated even more. Between 2002 and 2006 an astounding 75 percent of all economic growth was captured by the top

1 percent of income earners. And while the average 401(k) lost 25 percent between 2008 and 2009, the wealthiest 400 Americans became $30 billion richer."[1]

Yet the idea that the very wealthy should be penalized through excessive taxation is patently unfair to those who create wealth through investment and entrepreneurship. On a pragmatic level, it's an approach to taxation that would backfire by costing the nation dearly in terms of lost tax revenues.

Most people have no idea who in America is paying the real tax burden that funds the majority of government services, national defense, and virtually all the vast network of social welfare programs. The top 1 percent of American earners pay a staggering 40 percent of all federal taxes. The next 10 percent of earners pays another 40 percent of all federal taxes. This means that the top 11 percent of American earners pay 80 percent of the nation's taxes, supplying eight out of ten tax dollars to finance government programs. In addition, the bottom 60 percent of American earners pay virtually no federal income taxes, but they receive on average tens of thousands of dollars in income assistance annually through income assistance, welfare and other social programs, housing allowances, and food stamps, to name just a few.

The wealthy are the people who create wealth, and taking away their wealth through taxation will not solve America's problems. But the nation's top leadership has trouble understanding this. Not one member of President Obama's cabinet—including the president himself—has any private-sector job experience outside the ivory towers of academia. Even Timothy Geithner, the secretary of the Treasury, told the Senate during his nomination hearings that he had never had a regular job! The top leadership of this administration simply has no background or firsthand experience in the realm of entrepreneurial business. Thus they do not understand how wealth is created through the development of new products and services that people are willing to pay for. Neither do they seem to understand that as businesses create new products and services and consequently expand, they hire additional employees. These employees earn wages and pay taxes and buy consumer goods. All of this is good for the economy.

President Obama and his top advisors, however, are far more familiar with spending taxpayer money. I should add that President Obama has close ties to organized labor dating back to his college days. During his short tenure in the U.S. Senate, he had the most liberal voting record of any of his colleagues.

The argument in favor of imposing a heavier tax burden on the rich comes from socialist thinking. The pro-tax movement believes that those who earn a large income need to share more of their wealth with those who have less. The tax advocates fail to understand that only those who wisely earn and accumulate wealth are in a position to invest in the expansion of American businesses, either directly by owning their own businesses or by providing capital to promising companies through the purchase of stock or mutual funds.

President Obama's agenda is explicitly socialist. When he was running for president, he had a conversation with Joe Wurzelbacher, a blue-collar midwesterner who became famous as "Joe the Plumber." In October 2008, Obama said to Joe, "I think when you spread the wealth around, it's good for everybody."[2] The president has constantly spoken of raising the tax levels for those whom he defines as "the rich."

But raising the tax rates imposed on the rich in a free economy does not work out the way socialist-minded politicians imagine. Instead of passively agreeing to be taxed at higher rates, a great number of high earners and big investors vote with their feet. Rather than give more of their money to the government, they find alternative ways to invest and do business that are protected from higher levels of taxation.

Long gone are the days when Americans would tolerate being fleeced by higher tax rates just because they succeeded in earning and accumulating wealth. As a case study, look at what is happening in the states that have chosen to increase their taxes on the wealthy. When state governments decide to tax the rich, those entrepreneurs who produce wealth choose to move to states that have lower or no taxes. This has occurred in New York, New Jersey, California, Maryland, and many other states.

In Maryland, the Democrat state government failed to balance its 2009 budget. As a result, the legislature doubled the income tax rate on residents who earned more than $1 million annually. Those earning in excess of $1 million faced a 9.45 percent marginal state and local income tax rate. When these residents added that to the 36 percent federal rate, plus 6 percent for Social Security and Medicare, the high earners faced a top marginal combined tax rate of more than 50 percent. What hardworking person wants to give the government more than 50 percent of his or her income?

Despite the assurances of numerous politicians and the editors of the *Baltimore Sun,* who praised the higher taxes and predicted the state's top earners would "grin and bear it," many of the wealthy left the state. The number of taxpayers with million-dollar incomes in Maryland dropped more than 30 percent in just one year. Politicians had predicted the tax grab would increase tax revenues by $106 million; however, the state of Maryland collected $100 million *less* revenue than it did the year before, even though the tax rate for top incomes was far higher.

The Unjust American Tax Code

In 1969, the printed edition of the U.S. tax code filled 16,500 pages. By 2007, the code took up 67,506 pages. When you fill out your tax return, if you still do it on paper, you use the Form 1040 instruction booklet, which alone is 155 pages long.

The tax code has been corrupted by the efforts of tireless lobbyists who have convinced the members of Congress to bury thousands of tax-free clauses deep in the maze of this impossibly complex code. Even tax accountants, tax attorneys, and IRS officials are at a loss to explain fully all the complicated rules, requirements, exemptions, exceptions, adjustments, and extenuating eventualities.

To say that the U.S. tax code is impossible to understand is like saying the Atlantic Ocean is slightly damp. The tax code is not just incomprehensible, it is written in a way that is deliberately vague and confusing so that the tax advantages enjoyed only by those in favored categories are virtually invisible, hidden deep within the complexities of the document. This means that tinkering with the tax code will not solve the systemic problem; the only workable solution is to simplify the tax code so it can be printed in its entirety on one or two sheets of paper. Some form of a simplified flat tax is the only practical solution. Yet this will be vigorously resisted by tax accountants and lawyers, lobbyists for major corporations, and the politicians who gain political advantage by adding loopholes into the tax code.

For example, General Electric (GE) is one of the largest and most prosperous companies in America. In a November 17, 2011, blog in the *Weekly Standard,* John McCormack revealed that GE "filed a whopping 57,000-page federal tax return earlier this year but didn't pay taxes on

$14 billion in profits" in 2010. It was all legal but involved the use of hundreds of tax loopholes and obscure deductions as well as generous tax credits. GE was rewarded for making investments in low-income housing, financing so-called green energy projects, corporate research and development expenses, and depreciation of property.[3]

Rampaging Inflation Will Cripple the Economy

President Obama and Federal Reserve chairman Ben Bernanke do not want anyone to suspect there are any increases in the economic evil known as inflation. During his first four years in office, Bernanke's penchant for printing money drowned America in more new cash than was created during the twenty-six-year period from 1959 to 1985. As a result of this inflated money supply, very soon we will begin to see the first signs of aggressive inflation—anticipated to be around 10 percent. From 2013 through 2016 things will get much worse. Here is one reason why this is inevitable. When a nation hits 10 percent inflation, a ten-year Treasury bond will lose almost half its value. If inflation hits 20 percent, the remaining value of T-bills is negated. So those who hold shares of America's debt, so to speak, will be left holding worthless investments. Inflation steals wealth from all of us.

As for interest rates in the near future, there is no question they will be going up. Higher interest rates will weaken the stock market through lower profit margins, lower dividends, and a serious impact on the ability of businesses to hire additional employees. The worst-case scenario is that we could see as much as a 60 percent drop in the stock market and an unemployment rate as high as 30 percent.

Starting in 2007, America has endured a chain reaction of financial crashes. The housing market crumbled, then the stock market imploded. These collapsed bubbles were followed by the private-debt crash and its inevitable consequence: the implosion of consumer spending. Many Americans continue to struggle to rebuild their financial lives.

Mortgage foreclosures are expected to rise by 20 percent in 2012. At the same time, home values continue to drop. Homeowners face the prospect of losing 5 to 8 percent of their home's value by the end of 2012. In the long term, we face the risk of a massive housing collapse, possibly worse than the first housing crisis. Housing expert Robert Shiller believes home prices could fall another 25 percent within five years.

Underlying all of this is the financial fallout that will follow runaway inflation. Economic Armageddon will bring a crippling rise in inflation that will destroy most people's savings and investments. In addition, escalating government debt will force severe cutbacks in most of the social safety nets that so many Americans have come to rely on. Those who expect to have a cushion available to soften the blow during tough economic times will be disappointed.

It is too late to save America from the consequences of past economic practices and policies. Economic Armageddon will be long and painful, but it also could give rise to a renewal of the American spirit and the republican principles of limited government. New legislation and even constitutional amendments could be enacted to prevent future politicians from spending money that does not exist.

Regardless of how bad the economy gets, America eventually will recover. For now, the best thing to do is to be informed and to start making plans for you and your family.

4

A Defense of American Exceptionalism

*Christian Principles That Made America
Stand Above All Other Nations*

In addition to the widespread suffering that Americans have not faced since the Great Depression, the coming Economic Armageddon will remove America from its place of influence in the world. This is doubly tragic when you consider the reason why the United States gradually rose to a place of unrivaled power and influence in the world. America's Christian heritage and constitutional foundation—based on biblical principles—made it possible for the United States to gain influence and extend its reach around the globe.

While the founders were careful to follow the wisdom of Scripture in laying the nation's foundation, America's leaders in the latter part of the twentieth century chose to turn their backs on the founding principles that made this nation great. Underlying the coming economic collapse is the work of those who are dedicated to destroying capitalism, free enterprise, individual liberties, and limited government. These four things made America great, and they all were inspired by God's revealed truth.

Those who are dedicated to destroying America built a secularizing movement on one short phrase, "a wall of separation" between church and state, which is mentioned in an 1802 letter from Thomas Jefferson to some Baptist clergy in Danbury, Connecticut. It is astounding how much ground has been gained by secularists who have just four words, taken out of context, on which to base their argument.

Here is what they have conveniently overlooked: one phrase in one letter from the personal correspondence of just one of America's founders does not outweigh the clear purpose and intent of the official founding documents of our nation. Nor does it trump nearly 240 years of American history, which repeatedly shows that the United States has been blessed as a result of following divine principles derived from the Holy Scriptures.

Most history books emphasize the uniqueness of the American experiment by citing the decision to join representative democracy and capitalism. This political system gives all citizens a voice and most of them a vote while operating in concert with an economic system that encourages industry and initiative, innovation and hard work, risk and reward. All of this is true, but it is an incomplete explanation. It is impossible to explain America's greatness, its power and influence and unprecedented success, apart from its Christian origins.

However, the secularists refuse to acknowledge this fundamental aspect of America's history and how Christian faith has guided the life of the nation. Instead, they seize on a short phrase from a president's personal correspondence. They insist that Jefferson's four words carry sufficient weight to deny the clear truth about America. Secularists have worked tirelessly to exclude all expressions of faith and the influence of Christianity from the public square. Sadly, they have largely succeeded.

It is impossible to separate the causes of the nation's ills from decades of attacks on Christian belief and its expression. While the church-state debate has been a political hot potato for decades, we now see the anti-Christian forces for what they truly are: enemies of America. As part of the conspiracy to bring down the American Empire, the globalist elite use a misreading of the First Amendment to weaken the institutions that made America great. This is another front in the war against the American Empire, separate from attacks on the economy but doing just as much harm.

Looking at the Truth About America

We need to defend our nation against those who deny that God has chosen to use America to stand for the values and principles that build a God-honoring society. America is an exceptional nation in the history of the world. This exceptional standing is not based on the dedication and sacrifice of Americans dating back to the colonists or even the legendary "American ingenuity." These are important factors, of course, but the bigger truth is that America stands alone in human history because it is a nation that embodies the truths of the Scriptures. The French historian Alexis de Tocqueville wrote the book on American exceptionalism in 1835, titled *Democracy in America*. He identified unique American characteristics and practices that served as sources of the nation's greatness: a religious heritage, a commitment to law (especially the federalist system of recognizing states' rights), and a unique geography. These factors combined to make the United States stand apart and above the rest of the world.[1]

In an article in the *National Review*, Richard Lowry and Ramesh Ponnuru explained America's special character: "Our country has always been exceptional. It is freer, more individualistic, more democratic, and more open and dynamic than any other nation on earth. These qualities are the bequest of our Founding and of our cultural heritage. They have always marked America as special, with a unique role and mission in the world: as a model of ordered liberty and self-government and as an exemplar of freedom and a vindicator of it, through persuasion when possible and force of arms when absolutely necessary."[2]

The idea of American exceptionalism predates the founding of the United States. When President Ronald Reagan spoke of a "shining city on a hill," he was borrowing a phrase from John Winthrop, leader of a group of Puritans to the American colonies when they fled persecution in 1630. Winthrop told his fellow colonists, "We shall be as a city upon a hill. The eyes of all people are upon us."[3] Of course Winthrop had borrowed the inspired phrase from Matthew 5:14, in which Jesus tells His followers, "Ye are the light of the world. A city that is set on a hill cannot be hidden."

A Biblical Foundation Made America Great

To understand why the United States has been so important to the rest of the world, we need to consider its uniqueness. America's system of checks and balances, for instance, recognizes that human nature pushes leaders to exploit positions of power for personal gain and advantage. The damaging consequences of self-interest (growing out of original sin) are guarded against in the U.S. Constitution, with each branch of government responsible for one area of governance, and each branch possessing a check on the power of the other two. Adding an additional check against the abuse of power is the power that is granted to the American people.

Thus was created a unique system of self-government, forming a nation of people who were governed by "the consent of the governed," which is wording used in the Declaration of Independence. The result is a constitutional republic with individual liberty, elected representatives, and limited government. This government's powers are confined to the proper defense of individual citizens in their pursuit of life, liberty, property, and happiness. In 1776 these were identified as inalienable rights endowed by God.

This unique republic guarded against tyranny by checking the power of each of the three branches of government. This unprecedented system created four limits as checks and balances: the Executive (the president and administration), the Legislature (the two houses of Congress), the Judicial (the Supreme Court), and individual citizens (who can give or withhold their consent). The intent was that each was to balance and limit the others. This system also guarded against the dangers of a pure democracy in which a simple majority (50 percent plus one) could install a tyranny. Instead, the founders established a new form of representative government based on law, not based on men. The founders kept in mind the Greek philosopher Plato's warning that an unrestricted democracy must ultimately result in a dictatorship.

Further, the founders designed the new nation as a bottom-up system of governance, with ultimate power residing with the people. America is a constitutional republic of limited government, with the governing authority designed as a decentralized system. This is another safeguard against tyranny. No elected official or centralized federal system would be allowed to lord it over the citizenry.

This grass-roots system, in which citizens appear to be at the bottom but in truth hold the reins of power, originated not with the founding fathers but in a phrase coined by John Wycliffe, the first person to translate the Bible into English. In the late fourteenth century, Wycliffe described the role of the Bible in the life of England: "This book [the Bible] shall make possible government of the people, by the people and for the people."[4] In Wycliffe's view, sincere Christians who were capable of internal moral self-government needed only limited outside help and direction to create a stable and just society. The adoption of this principle by America's founders was not merely good statecraft, but it was based on the inspired principles of the Scriptures.

Critics have tried to dismiss such principles as archaic and no longer suited to a modern society. But history proves the validity and durability of the founders' wisdom. The principles withstood the fiercest test possible when the Union split in 1861 and the young nation went to war against itself. Eighty-seven years after the signing of the Declaration of Independence, 7,058 Americans were killed during a three-day battle in southern Pennsylvania. President Abraham Lincoln, committed to preserving and restoring the Union, reaffirmed the truth and validity of the founding declaration: "We here highly resolve that these dead shall not have died in vain—that this nation, under God, shall have a new birth of freedom—and that government of the people, by the people, for the people, shall not perish from the earth."[5] America's most beloved president reaffirmed the unique American conception of limited republican government.

God was at work in the founding of America, and He guided the founders as they formulated the Declaration of Independence, the Articles of Confederation, and the U.S. Constitution. The patriots who established this unique republic could not have known that their experiment in representative democracy would give rise to a nation of unrivaled global economic, political, and military power. But we know today that their experiment demonstrated to the rest of the world that adopting and following God's principles would produce a prosperous, powerful, freedom-loving nation.

The Plain Facts on America as a Christian Nation

The psalmist said it best: "Blessed is the nation whose God is the LORD; and the people whom he hath chosen for his own inheritance" (33:12). The United States has been blessed far beyond any other modern nation, and the reason for that is clear.

The founding document of the United States of America is a political document, not a religious or philosophical treatise. However, when the founders were setting down the principles and absolutes that would guide the nation, the Bible was the leading text that guided them. The emigrants who left England carried the Bible with them on the ships sailing to the first colonies in Virginia. The one book that was found in almost every home in early America was the Word of God. The Scriptures were without doubt the most profound influence on the thinking and language of the colonists.

A leading example of this is found in the 1784 preamble to the New Hampshire Constitution: "Every individual has a natural and unalienable right to worship God according to the dictates of his own conscience, and reason…as morality and piety, rightly grounded on evangelical principles, will give the best and greatest security to government, and will lay in the hearts of men, the strongest obligations to due subjection; and as the knowledge of these is most likely to be propagated through a society by the institution of the public worship of the Deity."[6]

It is important to recognize the source of the principles that undergirded the founding documents and laws of the American republic. The source, even when not quoted directly, is the Bible. While political documents reflect multiple influences and often limit the scope of discussion to pragmatic issues of governance, there remain numerous instances of undeniable adherence to Holy Writ. Visitors to Washington DC see repeated evidence of the influence of the Bible, Jesus Christ, and Christianity. As they visit famous sights throughout the capital, they encounter numerous inscriptions, including the Ten Commandments and other scriptural quotations, and major works of art that depict scenes from the Bible.

Consider these inscriptions engraved on the Washington Monument. On the capstone is the Latin phrase *Laus Deo*, which translates as "Praise be to God." In addition, there are engraved scriptures; for example, "Holiness unto the Lord" (Zechariah 14:20), "Search the Scriptures" (John 5:39), and "The memory of the just is blessed" (Proverbs 10:7). Beyond inscriptions on monuments is the nation's motto, seen on all coins and currency: "In God We Trust."

The founding fathers were, for the most part, godly men who took the Bible and Christian principles seriously. While textbooks used today in the public schools downplay the influence of Christian belief on the founders, unbiased historians acknowledge the significant ways in which the Bible shaped the foundation of this unique nation. A surprising number of America's underlying legal principles can be found in God's laws as recorded by Moses in the book of Deuteronomy.

The early leaders of America were committed to biblically based and balanced education. The Bible repeatedly calls on believers to teach their children the precepts of the Scriptures. As a result, the American educational system was founded on the importance of learning and understanding the Word of God. The Ivy League universities were founded by Christians and based on biblical principles. The founding principle of Harvard University is revealed in its original statement of purpose, as declared in the 1636 Harvard University student handbook: "Let every student be plainly instructed and earnestly pressed to consider well: the main end of his life and studies is 'to know God and Jesus Christ, which is eternal life' (John 17.3), and therefore to lay Christ in the bottom, as the only foundation of all sound knowledge and learning. And seeing the Lord only giveth wisdom, let everyone seriously set himself by prayer in secret to seek it of Him (Prov. 2.3)."

The first 126 American colleges and universities were devoted to the glory of Christ and committed to the advancement of the gospel. Early American believers took the Bible seriously and embraced its command to train up their children in the way of the Lord.[7]

If we look back to the hundred or so Pilgrims who landed at Plymouth Rock in 1620, they were mostly committed Christians who believed that all law in the new colony should be based on "the consent of the governed." The Pilgrims created a government compact based on a conviction that almighty God and His written revelation was the foundation of all law and order. They believed that civil law without a moral basis related to the Bible was truly no law at all. These settlers, who traveled to the New World to escape religious and political persecution, created a compact in which all subsequent law would not be based upon the rule of a distant monarch. Rather, all law in the future would originate from "the consent of the governed." This concept of limited government based on the desires of the citizens had never before been attempted.

The declared purpose of the original colonists was to establish a new government based on the principles of the Bible. Significantly, James I of England signed the initial New England charter, which proclaimed this goal: "To advance the enlargement of Christian religion, to the glory of God Almighty."[8]

The Written Record of the Founders

In May 1775 delegates representing each of the thirteen colonies met to discuss the future governance of a free and independent nation. Meeting at Carpenters' Hall in Philadelphia, at that time a quiet Pennsylvania town, the delegates included doctors, merchants, lawyers, and wealthy landowners. It was an unlikely group to gather as the nucleus of the most significant revolutionary movement in history. These men possessed no common national consciousness or tradition. The new nation that they proposed to found had little organization, no significant industries, no treasury, and nothing in the way of a trained military (outside of citizen militias). It would be hard to name any other revolutionary movement that commenced with so little preparation and materials.

If all that were not enough of a challenge, up to 15 percent of the colonial population (250,000) did not support independence. At the end of the Revolutionary War, some 70,000 colonists (known as Loyalists) who had not supported independence fled the colonies, most of them moving north to the British colonies of Quebec (including at that time the territories of Quebec and Ontario) and Nova Scotia.

The Declaration of Independence in 1776 marked the birth of a unique nation, under God, that was destined for world leadership. Remarkably, the founders of America, when declaring their independence from the greatest empire of that day, simultaneously made a total declaration of dependence of the God of the universe. The Declaration of Independence closed with these words: "With a firm reliance on the protection of Divine Providence, we mutually pledge to each other our lives, our fortunes, and our sacred honor." The fifty-six signers were men who knew that success would require years of battle and struggle, while defeat would lead to death in war or hanging as traitors. Five of the signers were captured by the British and killed. Twelve lost their homes and nine others were killed in the war.[9]

The patriots warned future generations that genuine reverence for God was the spiritual foundation of the American Republic and that to forget this spiritual foundation would endanger the nation's future.[10] Tragically, the spiritual apostasy of our generation now threatens the future of America and has led to the coming economic collapse of the only nation founded "under God."

History shows that several times during the past two centuries, when America had lost its way, a spiritual revival occurred. These reawakenings reversed downward trends in the morals of U.S. society. Spiritual revival again and again led to a revival of the biblical spirit that made America great.

Is America a Christian Nation?

The United States was founded as a Christian nation. No other nation was founded explicitly as a limited republic based on divinely inspired principles from Scripture. Critics point out that many of the founders were not fully orthodox in their Christian beliefs. This point remains debatable. But arguments over whether George Washington and Thomas Jefferson were philosophical deists have no bearing on the central question, which is, What guided the founders in deciding which principles and commitments would define the new nation? Explicitly Christian principles, made public in the early writings of the founders, undergird the Declaration of Independence and the U.S. Constitution. Both of these foundational documents reflect an overt recognition of God and His activities in the world and the necessity of basing laws, liberties, and rights on His revealed moral law. The idea that America is a secular state, with a requirement that public policy be strictly separate from Christian belief, did not exist in 1776, nor when the Constitution and the Bill of Rights were enacted (1787). The truth is that the U.S. Constitution was written with the intent of perpetuating a Christian nation.[11]

When laypeople and religious leaders in Europe began in the early sixteenth century to read the Holy Scriptures in their own language, a spiritual reformation followed. This was an early "back to the Bible" movement that overthrew the nonbiblical traditions of priests and the medieval church. As laypeople began to read the Scriptures in their own language they discovered how spiritually corrupt the medieval church had become. This opening of the Scriptures to the laity created a spiritual reformation that transformed Northern European society. The simultaneous development in 1520 of Johannes Gutenberg's movable type made it possible for inexpensive copies of the Bible to be placed in the hands of millions of Christians, leading to a spiritual reformation. Suddenly those who could read the Bible for themselves were discovering personal Christian faith, which was defined by a personal relationship with Jesus Christ.[12]

The emphasis in the Reformation on the priesthood of all believers helped the principles of Scripture to become universally known. A significant book was written in 1644 by Samuel Rutherford, a Presbyterian pastor, titled *Lex Rex* ("The Law and the Prince"). The earlier fundamental principle of government had been the medieval concept of the divine right of kings. Rutherford, however, presented a revolutionary principle based on the Word of God. He declared that the basis of law should be the principles of Scripture rather than human traditions. He declared that all people, even nobles and monarchs, were subject to the law of God.

In America, John Witherspoon, who taught the political principles of Samuel Rutherford, was the only minister of the gospel who signed the Declaration of Independence. Another key legal and political thinker was the respected jurist William Blackstone, whose writings established the principle that every law and right comes ultimately from God. The founders believed that all absolute rights mentioned in the Constitution are based on God's revelation in the Bible.

To this day, on every January 20 following a presidential election, the newly elected head of state stands in front of the national Capitol to take the oath of office. The president places a hand on the Bible. This tradition was begun by George Washington, who swore his oath of office with his hand on the Bible, along with a prayer, "So help me God."

The American experiment showed the rest of the world that a

country founded on God's principles prospers as it preserves freedom and opportunity for all its citizens. The thirteen colonies that came together to declare independence from foreign tyranny grew to become the most powerful nation on earth. But America's leaders lost sight of the commitments, values, and absolutes that made the nation great.

After World War II, the United States assumed the role of defender of freedom around the world. As the leader of the free world, America committed its military forces around the globe. The American military has been present to defend its allies and to oppose the expansionist ambitions of its enemies. But the American Empire is now facing its greatest enemy.

America's prosperity is being overwhelmed by suffocating national debt. At the same time, the U.S. military is recognizing that a nation in financial crisis cannot continue to serve as the world's policeman. The irony of being the world's leading military power is that your nation can be defeated from within. In the next chapter we will look at the military dominance of the American Empire and the dramatic changes that will come as a result of the nation's economic collapse.

The Strategy to Undermine the U.S. Military

*Other Nations Relied on America's Protection;
Now We Are Paying the Price*

An empire, by definition, possesses power and exerts influence—and enjoys dominance—over a vast part of the world. Early in the formation and growth of the American Republic, its location was a distinct advantage. Separated from Europe by the Atlantic Ocean and occupying a resource-rich territory extending from Maine to Georgia, the new nation was sufficiently isolated to experience a level of security from other nations vying for power in the Old World. Unlike the long-established countries of Europe, America was situated on a landmass with plenty of territory to the west that was open for expansion.

As the nation grew in size, strength, and influence, its military became more and more important. Over time, the U.S. military extended its mission far beyond defending the shores of America. After helping the Allies defeat the Axis nations in World War II, the United States was recognized as the most powerful military force in the world. Following the war, the United States assumed the role of global policeman.

According to the Pentagon, the U.S. military maintains some 716 overseas bases and installations in approximately 150 nations. (That number might be closer to 1,000 installations when hundreds of secret bases—such as unmanned drone launch sites—are included.) In 2011, the U.S. Department of Defense had a base budget of $530 billion, with an additional $160 billion to fund Overseas Contingency Operations (the Obama administration's term for the War on Terror). The combined U.S. military budget of almost $700 billion exceeds the defense spending of the next ten nations combined.

The U.S. Navy has eleven aircraft carriers, ten of which are *Nimitz*-class carriers, the largest warships in the world. Spain and Italy have two carriers each, while Britain, France, Russia, India, Brazil, and Thailand each have one. China purchased an aircraft carrier from Russia and is retrofitting it; however, it still has to acquire naval aircraft and its pilots need to be trained for carrier operations. A U.S. Navy aircraft carrier battle group normally consists of a single aircraft carrier surrounded by nuclear-powered submarines and numerous *Aegis*-class destroyers equipped with cruise missiles. The carrier groups allow America to mobilize sea and air power and long-range attack capabilities nearly anywhere in the world.

The Military Reach of the American Empire

Throughout history, empires have risen and gradually declined. Some of them expanded too far from their home territory, so that they could no longer keep soldiers armed and well supplied. Others became lax in discipline or resolve. The result was that declining empires grew vulnerable to other rising military and political powers—opposing nations that were flexing their muscles in battle against the formerly dominant power. In the case of the British Empire, as we have seen, after World War II, Great Britain withdrew from many of the areas it had colonized.

In the case of the American Empire, few rival powers would be foolish enough to risk a direct military confrontation. As we have seen, there is no lack of resolve in the U.S. military. Nor is there a reluctance to make use of the latest in weaponry and military technology in seeking out and attacking an enemy. So America is not likely to be weakened by a direct attack against its defenses. Instead, any effort to drain power from the United States—and, by extension, from its military force—has to be done indirectly. In the case of the American Empire, the military is being attacked through the weakening of the U.S. economy.

The massive economic downturn and mounting public debt create problems that reach far beyond business, investment, unemployment, and a new housing crisis. The debt problems also are leading to the weakening of the U.S. military, which over time will impede the country's ability to defend the nation's shores. Before that can happen, the downsized armed forces will no longer have a global military presence to protect U.S. interests overseas. Already the Obama administration is proposing that the federal deficit be addressed by making significant reductions to the Department of Defense budget. The president would prefer to make deep cuts in the Pentagon budget to help shrink the deficit rather than cut back on waste and reduce entitlement programs.

One mark of the American Empire is the post–World War II role of global policeman assumed by the United States. It is astoundingly expensive to maintain a significant military presence around the globe, presenting an economic challenge even for a superpower. The defense budget of the United States accounts for nearly 43 percent of the world's combined military expenditures. However, a significant portion of defense expenditures are concealed in top-secret so-called black budget programs.

For the sake of comparison, consider the military budget of the last global empire, Great Britain. At the height of its international ascendancy, when Britain had colonized almost a quarter of the world, the British Empire maintained military bases in 35 foreign nations.[1] Far exceeding that number, the U.S. military maintains some 716 bases and installations in approximately 150 nations.[2]

America is the only nation that can mobilize and deploy its armed forces through the air with both manned and unmanned aircraft, on the ocean, in the ocean, and on land. The American military can strike quickly because it can transport massive numbers of troops and matériel by air.

The Pentagon does not list the full range and reach of all its land-based military outposts, bases, and other installations. For instance, the Pentagon does not acknowledge military or intelligence bases in numerous nations, including Israel, Kuwait, Qatar, unspecified nations in Africa, and central Asia. Not included in its list of official bases are secret espionage bases, such as an air base in Qatar, from which the U.S. military wages effective unmanned drone warfare.[3]

A list of the major military bases, listening posts, missile and artillery test ranges, weapons depots, staging areas, naval seaports, shipyards, and intelligence installations forms an impressive catalog of the American Empire's military reach and power. No other world empire in history could rival America's military might. Unlike previous empires such as France, Russia, and Britain, the high-tech, highly sophisticated military forces of the American Empire are capable of projecting massive military power at a few hours' notice virtually anywhere on the globe. U.S. troops were fighting Al Qaeda terrorists throughout the Afghan mountains within weeks of the 9/11 attacks in New York and Washington DC.

The American military also surpasses its rivals with an ability to launch precision attacks. Laser-guided missiles can deliver either nuclear or conventional warheads into a cave opening or through the door or window of a targeted building. These projectiles can be launched from up to two thousand miles away, or they can be deployed in the most low-tech manner imaginable.

In 2001, U.S. Special Forces rode into battle on horseback with wireless GPS laser designators to direct cruise missiles toward targets in Afghanistan. After reconnaissance forces detected a target, such as an arms depot, an Al Qaeda cave, or a fortified building in a village, the Special Forces operatives entered the target's GPS coordinates into a laptop and sent the target's location via satellite to drones circling thirty thousand feet overhead. The information was relayed first to a military command post in Saudi Arabia and then transferred to military personnel in the United States. Air force personnel at places such as Nellis Air Force Base in Nevada would then launch drones from an airbase on the island of Diego Garcia in the Indian Ocean to the target.

If that is not the work of a world empire, what is? No other empire in history possesses such capabilities. America takes pride in its global watchdog role, but financing such a force and supplying it with the weapons, equipment, and technology that fulfills this mission is one of the factors contributing to the coming economic collapse.

Strategies to Defeat an Unrivaled Military Power

Department of Defense spending is the largest item in the federal budget, totaling $693 billion in 2010. After the terrorist attacks of September 11, 2001, U.S. military and homeland security spending increased by more than 120 percent.

With defense consuming such a huge portion of federal spending, some taxpayers will soon rebel. Not only does the spending seem out of proportion to the threat, but it seems misguided when so many citizens are suffering from declining home values, diminished retirement funds, high unemployment, and a challenging economy for doing business. All of this makes it easy for them to blame military spending for being wasteful.

"With Americans sending more tax dollars to Washington and getting less in return, they will be less generous in supporting not only defense spending, but also diplomacy, foreign aid and the other tools of U.S. foreign policy," said Michael Mandelbaum of the Johns Hopkins School of Advanced International Studies. "A smaller defense budget and less ambitious international commitments won't necessarily herald the end of America's era as a global superpower. But they do mean that we will have to be much more selective about where and how we deploy our military and diplomatic resources."[4]

Pressures are growing to cut the federal deficit by trimming defense appropriations. Pentagon budget reductions would mean, among other cutbacks, consolidating or closing many overseas bases. A study by the Center for American Progress recommends cutting U.S. troop strength in Europe and Asia by one-third by 2016. Reducing troop strength and cutting back on overseas military installations would constitute a partial withdrawal of the American Empire from the world stage, but the effects would reach far beyond that. Budget reductions, cutbacks on military personnel, and base closings would have a dramatic impact on overall U.S. foreign policy.

"In a cash-strapped era, the kind of operations we've launched since the end of the Cold War are increasingly unaffordable," Mandelbaum said. "From Somalia through Haiti and the Balkans and into Iraq and Afghanistan, America's recent military interventions have sprung from a variety of motives but produced a common result: All entangled the United States in the frustrating, protracted and expensive task of nation-building."[5]

Former U.S. Defense Secretary Robert Gates warned Congress that closing bases overseas could communicate to the world that America is losing interest in maintaining a strategic advantage. "The biggest policy question that has to be asked is what kind of signal do you want to send the rest of the world," he told a Senate appropriations committee. "Are we basically sending the message to the rest of the world—to China, to Iran, to North Korea—that the U.S. is closing up and heading home? What kind of a role do you want for the United States in the world?"[6]

Following the dissolution of the USSR in 1991 and the reduction in Russia's political, economic, and military power, many commentators believed that the world was entering a period of globalization and world peace. It was said that the United States was the unquestioned victor in the Cold War, having achieved economic and military domination of the world.

The idea arose that the United States was now the "indispensible nation," positioned to provide global leadership. This development would usher in a new world order that would spread the American values of liberty, democracy, and human rights, together with the economic freedoms essential to achieve prosperity, around the world. America's global presence and influence were unlikely to be challenged.

The respected political scientist Francis Fukuyama wrote about "the end of history," by which he meant that the rise of U.S. military hegemony had transformed the world by limiting the possibility of major wars. Fukuyama argued that the triumph of American democratic capitalism was the concluding stage in the evolution of Western political economic development.

High-Tech Weapons Systems to Be Used in the Last Days

On November 17, 2011, the United States successfully tested a hypersonic bomb that could be launched from any military base in the continental United States. This weapon travels more than five times the speed of sound (3,805 mph at sea level) and can cover thousands of miles to hit a designated military target. The warhead can strike anywhere on the planet within one hour. The hypersonic weapon has the potential to fly at a relatively flat trajectory within the atmosphere, rather than soaring upward and leaving the atmosphere as a ballistic missile would do.[7]

The hypersonic weapon was developed by a Pentagon research group known as the Defense Advanced Research Projects Agency (DARPA).

The Army's advanced hypersonic weapon was launched from the Pacific Missile Range Facility on the island of Kauai in Hawaii using a three-stage booster system. It eventually splashed down in the Ronald Reagan Ballistic Missile Defense Test Site near Kwajalein Atoll.

In future wars, nations will enter the field of battle with weapons so advanced they will seem to come straight out of a science fiction story. Such weapons systems will transform the way wars are fought and will make possible not only selective killing but also will assure more widespread devastation.

These ominous developments make it clear, in light of biblical prophecy, that we are witnessing the beginning of the predicted last-days events. Technology is being developed for use in warfare but also for controlling and limiting the movement, choices, and freedom of thought of people. Both types of technology will come into play with the rise of a global government and the coming of the Antichrist. The Antichrist's totalitarian regime will make full use of these sophisticated tools of war and the technology of the total-surveillance society. We read in the prophecies of John in the book of Revelation that these technologies will be used during the seven-year Tribulation.

The Coming Global Government

Jesus Christ prophesied, "And there shall be signs in the sun, and in the moon, and in the stars; and upon the earth distress of nations, with perplexity; the sea and the waves roaring; men's hearts failing them for fear, and for looking after those things which are coming on the earth: for the powers of heaven shall be shaken" (Luke 21:25–26).

Thousands of years ago the Old Testament prophets foresaw a scale of war and the use of advanced weaponry that far exceeded anything known to humanity. For example, Jesus's prophecy in Luke 21 may refer to the use of nuclear weapons, which did not exist until the mid-twentieth century. In the Greek language, the word rendered in the Jerusalem Bible, Reader's Edition (RJB), as "heavens" is actually a reference to "the atom."

Similarly, the prophet John may have referred to the use of nuclear weapons: "And the heaven departed as a scroll when it is rolled together; and every mountain and island were moved out of their places" (Revelation 6:14). Using the descriptive language available to him, John depicts what appears to be a devastating thermonuclear blast that destroys mountains and islands in a way that could be accomplished only by the use of nuclear weapons.

The prophet Zechariah may have referred to neutron bombs in his prophecy regarding the attack on the city of Jerusalem at the end of the Battle of Armageddon. "And this shall be the plague wherewith the LORD will smite all the people that have fought against Jerusalem; their flesh shall consume away while they stand upon their feet, and their eyes shall consume away in their holes, and their tongue shall consume away in their mouth" (Zechariah 14:12). The prophet's description that "their flesh shall consume away" would accurately describe the terrible effect of neutron bomb radiation that emits massive amounts of gamma rays that destroy flesh without vaporizing bones, buildings, or equipment. Only the victim's skeleton remains while nearby buildings and equipment are left undamaged.

Isaiah appears to have foreseen the development of airplanes. He prophesied about God defending Jerusalem in the generation of the last days. The prophet described the methods of defense with the phrases "as birds flying" and "passing over he will preserve it." Five centuries before the birth of Christ, Isaiah wrote, "As birds flying, so will the LORD of hosts defend Jerusalem; defending also he will deliver it; and passing over he will preserve it" (Isaiah 31:5).

This prophecy was fulfilled in 1917. In December of that year, as the Allied Expeditionary Force approached Jerusalem and the Turkish army that controlled the city, Lord Edmund Allenby, a British general and committed Christian, ordered his small air force to fly over the Holy City. Pilots dropped pamphlets that warned Turkish soldiers to flee the city. Fortunately, rather than fight out a deadly street-by-street battle, the Turks fled Jerusalem. Thus both the city and the civilian population of Jews, Muslims, and Christians were saved from the horror of battle in the ancient city. Truly, God had defended His Holy City and preserved it through the unprecedented use of aircraft.

Prophecies that describe the terrible final worldwide conflict during the last days also seem to describe long-range ballistic missiles with nuclear warheads. John wrote, "And there fell a great star from heaven, burning as it were a lamp, and it fell upon the third part of the rivers, and upon the fountains of waters" (Revelation 8:10). This may be John's description of an incoming missile. The prophet Joel may also have described the use of a missile-based weapon: "A fire devoureth before them; and behind them a flame burneth" (Joel 2:3).

The apostle John, having never seen an armored vehicle, described what in his vision appears to be the use of tanks: "And thus I saw the horses in the vision, and them that sat on them, having breastplates of fire, and of jacinth, and brimstone: and the heads of the horses were as the heads of lions; and out of their mouths issued fire and smoke and brimstone. By these three was the third part of men killed, by the fire, and

by the smoke, and by the brimstone, which issued out of their mouths"
(Revelation 9:17–18). Modern tanks deliver high-explosive shells, and
their barrels also can act as flamethrowers.

Weapons That Kill Based on Ethnicity

With the decoding of the human genome, military scientists in many
nations may choose to develop genetic weapons of mass destruction.
One foreboding application of this science is to target specific populations that are perceived as a threat to the ruling powers while leaving
all other people unaffected by the weapon. In light of the terrible genocide of World War II, together with the more recent genocidal killing
of 800,000 of the Tutsi population of Rwanda in 1994, the danger is
overwhelming. Genetic research combined with advanced technology
in the development of future weapons of war could lead to the mass
destruction of entire ethnic populations. It is possible that future genetic
warfare may be one of the most terrible judgments of the Tribulation
period referred to by Daniel and John in their prophecies (see Daniel
9:26–27; Revelation 6–18).[8]

Nanotechnology and microfusion nuclear weapons

The U.S. military's ability to miniaturize weapons has led to the development of microfusion nuclear bombs. A range of military nanotechnology
weapons also has been developed, including micro-, low-yield nuclear
weapons. The United States, the United Kingdom, France, Russia,
China, and Israel have the ability to deploy mini-nuclear weapons, which
produce precise and devastating effects against an enemy military target.

Developments in weapons technology during the last two decades have played a significant role in setting the stage for the unprecedented wars to be fought in the last days. At the end of the Antichrist's period of global domination, a titanic battle will be waged between the enormous armies of the "kings of the east" (Revelation 16:12) and the armies of the west, led by the Antichrist.

The United States is absent from the Bible's prophetic descriptions of the events of the last days, including the titanic wars that will be waged. The lack of any mention of America's participation in these wars could indicate that not only will America be decimated by a cataclysmic economic meltdown but also that the United States' military forces will be so diminished that they will not be deployed beyond the borders of the country.

6

Your Future in the American Police State

The Federal Government Has Stolen Your Rights in the Name of Protecting You

As we have seen, the American Empire will fall with a suddenness that will catch most Americans off guard. It's not that there aren't a great number of signs pointing to it. The reason most people will be surprised is that they do not know how to read the signs.

The same is true when you finally realize how many of your constitutional liberties have been taken away. The theft of our rights has been gradual, and since 2001 it has taken place under the guise of combating terrorism. You could compare it to a parent telling a young child that the medicine might taste horrible, but it's for the child's good.

Is this reduction in personal liberty really for our own good, or are the same forces that are destroying America also using the threat of terrorism as a cover for controlling us? As the time of the Antichrist's appearance on the world stage draws near, the globalists who support a centralized world government know that it's necessary to install a system of some kind to control the citizenry.

That is what we see happening now in the nation that was founded on the principles of individual freedom. If we were to compare our lives today with the lives of early Americans in the late eighteenth century, the differences would go far beyond any advances in transportation, communication, and technology. Today, we are regulated, restricted, socially engineered, and constantly watched. Americans' lives are being limited and directed in ways that benefit the government but put individuals at a disadvantage. Beyond that, we are watched, monitored, and recorded around the clock. Today, you have to work at it to keep your thoughts secret.

Our government would have us believe that such monitoring of our movements and contacts with others is necessary. The rationale is that we have to be watched in order to be kept safe. In the process of monitoring ordinary citizens, the argument goes, the authorities have a better chance of uncovering the people who are plotting evil. This theft of our liberties was legislated largely in the aftermath of the terrorist attacks on New York and Washington DC on September 11, 2001. New laws granted expanded powers to law enforcement agencies and at the same time took away a good measure of the personal liberties of every American citizen. The government's rhetoric makes the Patriot Act and related legislation sound like a harmless, sensible response to the escalating threats against our nation. In practice, however, these security measures catch all of us in a net that robs us of privacy, freedom of movement, and the ability to carry on our lives as we see best.

Recent applications of technology work hand in hand with the government's goal of keeping tabs on the American people. Before email existed, when we were writing letters to conduct business and to keep current with personal relationships, it would have been impossible for the government to read every letter that was sent through the mail. But with the adoption of email, every message is intercepted and stored and, if needed, can be retrieved and viewed to find out what we communicate "in private."

The same is true of cell phones. Before cell phones were in wide use, the government could listen in on phone calls via wiretaps. But a person could always choose to use a different phone (including a pay phone) to avoid such electronic eavesdropping. Now, with cell phones, not only are our conversations out there for Big Brother to listen in on, but our location is pinpointed. If the authorities want to find you, they can.

These examples point to what's obvious to all: if you use the Internet for research and email and cell phones for texts and calls, you are sharing your private life with the world. You can protect your privacy to an extent by staying off those networks or living "off the grid." But that is far from enough to protect your rights.

The Government's Obsession with Security

If you should be suspected of terrorist intentions or activities—or if you are suspected of being sympathetic to or in contact with possible terrorists—you are of great interest to the federal government. An astonishing 1,271 government organizations and 1,931 private companies are working on a wide range of programs related to counterterrorism, homeland security, and intelligence. These personnel operate out of approximately 10,000 locations across the United States. The *Washington Post* discovered that an estimated 854,000 people hold top-secret security clearances.

The Pentagon's Defense Intelligence Agency grew from 7,500 employees in 2002 to 16,500 today. The budget of the National Security Agency (NSA), which conducts electronic eavesdropping around the globe, has doubled. The thirty-five FBI Joint Terrorism Task Forces have grown to 106.

Twenty-four new security and intelligence organizations were created in 2001, including the Office of Homeland Security with its 230,000-person workforce and the Foreign Terrorist Asset Tracking Task Force. In 2002, thirty-seven more agencies were created to track weapons of mass destruction, collect threat tips, and coordinate a worldwide focus on counterterrorism. During 2003 another thirty-six organizations were formed, followed by another twenty-six in 2004. (But that did not end the expansion of counterinsurgency, intelligence-gathering, eavesdropping, and surveillance activities. Such agencies increased by thirty-one in 2005, with thirty-two more in 2006 and at least twenty more added each year in 2007, 2008, and 2009.)

Here is where things get personal. American citizens are unknowingly planting listening devices—and worse—in their own homes by using web-connected devices. Without knowing it, when people download a movie or television show from Netflix or a similar online service, or they listen to Internet radio, they may be allowing unknown and unwanted watchers to know what they are doing and where they are. According to David Petraeus, the director of the Central Intelligence Agency

(CIA), "Spies will no longer have to plant bugs in your home. The rise of 'connected' gadgets controlled by apps will mean that people 'bug' their own homes."[1] He added, "Items of interest will be located, identified, monitored, and remotely controlled through technologies such as radio-frequency identification, sensor networks, tiny embedded servers, and energy harvesters—all connected to the next-generation internet using abundant, low-cost, and high-power computing."[2]

Rob Waugh reported on Mail Online that a computer chip company, ARM, had created inexpensive, low-powered computer chips that will be used in everything from refrigerators and ovens to doorbells. ARM's chips are smaller and much cheaper than previous computer processors, and they are designed to add an Internet connection to virtually every kind of electrical appliance in a home. Those who study future technologies and their impact on our society "think that one day 'connected' devices will tell the Internet where they are and what they are doing at all times," wrote Waugh, "and will be mapped by computers as precisely as Google Maps charts the physical landscape now."[3]

Surveillance devices often are marketed to corporations for legitimate uses. For instance, many large energy companies use surveillance drones to monitor the condition of remote assets such as oil rigs and miles of oil and gas pipelines. Typically, these are small helicopter drones, weighing about five and a half pounds and small enough to fit into the trunk of a car.

However, the history of constantly evolving technology is that every useful device can be miniaturized. The company AeroVironment announced that it had developed tiny hummingbird-sized drones that can be used for surveillance and spying. Many believe that within a few years the scale of surveillance robots will shrink to the size of a housefly. This technology could be used to infiltrate and monitor enemy installations and terrorist cells without detection.

Of course, devices that are developed with a military or antiterrorism purpose in mind can also be used to monitor ordinary citizens. While such uses of these technologies violate the Constitution, it is easy for Washington to rationalize that it is necessary for national security. With terror threats increasing, our constitutional rights are the least of Washington's worries. In fact, there are elements in the government that are convinced that denying citizens their right to privacy is critical to ensuring the security of the nation. This includes the right to free inquiry, the right to private communication, and the right to oppose government policy without fear of reprisal or being subjected to greater scrutiny. Add to this the denial of individual rights, the elevation of antiterror and national security concerns over constitutionally guaranteed rights, and the accelerated expansion of centralized control from Washington. All of these are hastening the dismantling of the American Empire.

The American Empire Has Turned Against Its Own

In generations past it was assumed that the federal government used advances in surveillance, weaponry, and law enforcement to guard against crime and protect the nation's borders. But the government has shifted much of its attention away from defending against an outside threat and toward monitoring ordinary citizens on U.S. soil. Here are some examples of technology that is being used against us.

President Obama signed the National Defense Authorization Act in 2011, which allows the indefinite detention of American citizens by the U.S. military anywhere around the world. This astonishing attack on fundamental constitutional rights codified yet another facet of the imperial presidency despite the president's assertion that he would never invoke the law.[4]

The National Defense Authorization Act not only provided funding for the military, it also violated the U.S. Constitution. Why, in an appropriations bill, was it necessary to trod on a citizen's right of protection against unlawful detention? The questionable provisions of the law were presented as necessary steps to enable the arrest and detention of suspected terrorists, including American citizens.

Although President Obama threatened to veto this bill because he claimed he opposed the provisions, in the end he signed it into law. He chose to do this on the last day of the year, when few reporters or news commentators were paying attention. Previously he had objected to the military's exercising these powers, so Congress added provisions that transferred the ultimate authority to detain suspects from the military to the president. Civilian law enforcement, including the FBI, still has the authority to investigate terrorism.

The real danger to American freedom includes the possibility of detaining citizens and holding them in military custody, without trial, for as long as there is a war on terror. It's bad enough that these draconian police state powers apply to foreign terrorists under the provisions of the Patriot Act, but it is an enormous step toward the complete loss of liberty to have such authority now extend to the apprehension and indefinite incarceration of any American suspected of supporting terrorism. The grounds for suspicion are broad and vague. You can fall under suspicion if you donate money to an organization the government deems to be a threat to America. Anthony Romero, executive director of the American Civil Liberties Union, warned, "The statute is particularly dangerous because it has no temporal or geographic limitations, and can be used by this and future presidents to militarily detain people captured far from any battlefield."[5]

The Hidden, Parallel U.S. Government

The proliferation of nuclear weapons and the increase in terror threats to the United States required the federal government to create contingency plans to survive an attack on Washington DC that involved weapons of mass destruction. These plans address the question of how the government would continue to operate if key targets in the nation's capital were obliterated. The result is an extensive underground government structure. The reserve government would operate out of subterranean military and government continuity bases scattered throughout the United States. Some studies claim that as many as twenty-six underground cities exist where backup government functions run in parallel to the conventional government. Former cabinet members from both parties have been trained to act at a moment's notice in the event of an attack. They are prepared to carry on the essential government functions. In addition, backup personal and computers operate a parallel financial system to provide continuity and guarantee the integrity of the stock exchange, commodity markets, the banking system, and many other essential market functions.

The continuity-of-government program was created in response to the attacks of September 11, 2001. Provisions include the succession of leadership, continuity planning as described above, and the basic logistics related to essential governmental operations. According to the *Washington Post*, the backup government is so large that virtually no one can calculate how much it costs, how many people it employs, or how many programs and agencies are represented.[6]

Given the threat of terrorist attacks, hostile military actions taken by enemy nations, and the threat of weapons of mass destruction, it's understandable on one level that the federal government would make provisions for the continuity of governance. However, the reasons for activating this second-tier government are not limited to times of military threat or attack. "When COOP [Continuity of Operations] planners discuss emergencies, disasters, or adverse events they can refer to any incident that could result in the inability of a vital governmental entity or agency to provide essential services to its constituents, taxpayers, citizens, businesses, and visitors," wrote two reporters for the *Washington Post*. An emergency could be invoked that falls far short of what most people would categorize as an immediate national threat. Just by declaring that such an emergency exists, the parallel government could be set into motion.[7]

A two-year investigation by the *Washington Post* discovered the enormous, top-secret operational government that is hidden from the public. Further, this underground government functions without any meaningful congressional oversight. After nine years of planning and implementation and billions of dollars in funding, the system is so massive that no one can provide an effective oversight or even assess its effectiveness. In other words, a structure that was set up to protect us is so secretive that no legitimate authority is able to control it. "The top-secret world the government created in response to the terrorist attacks of Sept. 11, 2001, has become so large, so unwieldy and so secretive that no one knows how much money it costs, how many people it employs, how many programs exist within it."[8]

For instance, fifty-one separate federal organizations and military commands operating in fifteen cities track the flow of funds that are going to and from suspected terrorist networks. The massive duplication of work by multiple analysts who attempt to make sense of documents as well as wiretapped and computer conversations obtained by foreign and domestic spying share their judgments by publishing a reported fifty thousand intelligence reports each year, a volume so large that many reports are routinely ignored.

This overload of intelligence information has led to a few terrorist disasters, such as the killing of thirteen members of the U.S. military and the wounding of thirty-two more at Fort Hood in Texas by a Muslim soldier, U.S. Army Major Nidal Malik Hasan. Hasan should have been red-flagged for his associations as well as his suspect behavior. He had exchanged emails with a well-known radical Muslim cleric in Yemen who was being monitored by U.S. intelligence.[9]

Each day, the collection systems run by the National Security Agency intercept and store 1.7 billion emails, phone calls, and fax communications, plus other types of electronic communications. The $1.8 billion National Geospatial Intelligence Agency, which analyzes images and mapping data of the earth, is home to eighty-five hundred employees. In Anacostia, Virginia, a suburb of Washington DC, a $3.4 billion complex is being built for the Department of Homeland Security. The new headquarters will be the largest government complex built since the Pentagon was constructed during World War II.

How the Imperial Presidency Violates Your Conscience

The federal government's trampling of individual rights goes far beyond the surveillance of private citizens and the operation of extensive hidden government operations that escape congressional oversight. President Obama took the extraordinary step of unilaterally abrogating federal law so he could violate the moral convictions of millions of Americans. In spite of the White House's promise that provisions of the Affordable Care Act (also referred to as Obamacare) would not violate federal conscience laws, actions by the president and the Department of Health and Human Services quickly broke that promise.

On January 20, 2012, the Department of Health and Human Services announced regulations that would compel practically all employers, including many religious organizations and religiously affiliated institutions, to include in their health insurance policies Food and Drug Administration (FDA)–approved methods of contraception. The regulations would provide no exemptions or protections for religiously affiliated institutions, including Catholic charities, hospitals, and universities. The only concession made for organizations that oppose having to pay for contraception—and they will pay for it through the increased premiums for their employees whether they use the insurance coverage or not—is that these organizations were given an additional year, until August 2013, to comply. The practical effect of this extension was an additional twelve months' delay in the enforcement of the law.[10]

This mandated contraceptive coverage in health insurance plans, including those offered by religiously affiliated employers, is a direct violation of the First Amendment's guarantee of freedom of religious expression and noninterference of government in matters of conscience. Under the regulation, all religious institutions that employ workers, except churches, are required to offer health insurance that includes free prescription contraception and coverage for sterilization and drugs that induce the abortion of a fertilized ovum, even when the employer opposes these acts on religious grounds.

The arbitrary bureaucratic decisions of the Obama administration raise the following issues that should deeply disturb every freedom-loving American:

1. Contraception, sterilization, and abortion pills are to be classi-fied as medical prevention. The legal authority for this unconsti-tutional measure is the secretary of Health and Human Services. But categorizing pregnancy as a disease equivalent is a value de-cision being presented to the public as a scientifically grounded medical decision. If contraception is the same as disease preven-tion, then what are fertility clinics? Producers of disease?

2. Pregnancy prevention will be free to all with no required copay-ment. Why? Is contraception now judged to be morally superior to legitimate medical treatments such as the use of penicillin to combat infection?

3. The exemptions for religious institutions extend only to churches, not to church-run hospitals and charities or to re-ligiously affiliated hospitals and colleges. The secretary of the Department of Health and Human Services shall determine whether church-operated organizations and ministries are protected by the First Amendment. President Obama's health-care reform measures deliberately violate the Roman Catholic Church's right to the free exercise of religion, which is guaran-teed by the First Amendment.

The executive branch of the federal government has no power under the Constitution to enact legislation. That power belongs to Congress. The deliberate violation of the First Amendment by the Obama admin-istration is yet another instance of the unconstitutional consolidation of power in the office of president.

This attack on the personal morals, religious convictions, and matters of conscience of millions of Americans is one of the most blatant acts of the federal government against its citizens, but it is far from the only one. A further indication of the disregard for rights guaranteed under the Constitution comes by way of a presidential executive order in March 2012.

The Executive Order of March 16, 2012

President Obama outdid himself when he signed the executive order titled National Defense Resources Preparedness. This executive order gives the executive branch the power to take over the government, to essentially consolidate all federal control, in a time of national emergency. Even more mind-boggling, the order gives the president the authority to determine when it is necessary to declare a national emergency.

The order grants the Department of Homeland Security, as well as the secretaries of Agriculture, Energy, Transportation, Defense, Commerce, Labor, and Health and Human Services broad, unilateral powers that invite unimaginable abuse. The heads of those federal departments are given control over essential resources, including the power to confiscate or redelegate materials, services, and facilities as deemed necessary or appropriate to promote the national defense.

While there are numerous laws on the books that grant virtual dictatorial powers to the president and the executive branch in the event of a national emergency, this executive order establishes a clear chain of command and control over all aspects of American life. If you have ever questioned whether we live in a police state, this outrage should remove any lingering doubts. This could be the final nail in the coffin, issuing a death notice for American liberty as the founders envisioned it.

Now, we will turn our attention from internal betrayals and violations to an overseas power that could bring America to its knees without a single act of aggression.

7

China's Strategy for Controlling the U.S. Economy

How a Foreign Nation Can Call the Shots Without Firing a Shot

When we examine the evidence that points to China's plan to bankrupt America, there is no need to fear overstatement. The plain facts are more than a little disturbing. The sobering truth is that China has such an aggressive economy that it is looking for places to invest internationally. By buying up U.S. debt and by investing heavily in American companies and natural resources, China can position itself to call the shots without firing a shot in anger.

Evidence compiled since 2010 by Porter Stansberry of Stansberry & Associates Investment Research, the largest investment research organization of its kind in the world, establishes that China has embarked on a covert economic plan that will extract billions of dollars from the United States. The financial media have virtually ignored this story, but you need to understand the serious risk this poses to the most important financial decisions you will make over the next few years.

China Purchased $1.5 Trillion in U.S. Treasury Bills

In the last few decades the Chinese government has purchased nearly $1.5 trillion dollars in U.S. Treasury bills. In addition to that amount, the Chinese government holds far more than $3 trillion worth of U.S. assets and securities when you add in U.S. bonds and physical dollar holdings. This staggering investment, made by buying up U.S. debt and dollars, represents hundreds of billions of dollars *more* than what the U.S. government collects annually in corporate and individual taxes. America can never hope to repay even the $1.5 trillion that China holds in Treasury bills. To be more specific, that level of debt owed to China can never be paid back by any normal means.

China's financial leaders know this, but the reality is that America and China are trapped in a mutually dependent economic relationship. While the U.S. government is faced with an enormous debt, the Chinese also are trapped by a huge outstanding loan they cannot simply write off as a bad debt. The debt America owes China is far too large for the Chinese government to absorb, but neither will they ever collect the balance that is owed them through any standard system of repayment.

Do not think the Chinese will be bighearted and simply forgive the debt. Instead, they developed an approach that protects them while also enabling them to deal with the financial crisis. The Chinese have launched a plan to reacquire as much of their borrowed money as possible. When China executes the plan it will extract enormous sums from the U.S. treasury as well as from ordinary American citizens.

China's Plan to Safeguard Its Own Economy

The Chinese government has taken strategic steps to protect the value of China's currency. Meanwhile, the Chinese government is engaged in a full-scale currency war with the United States to destroy the value of the U.S. dollar. The strategy is fairly simple. The amounts paid for all purchases of Chinese exports are, by law, paid to the Chinese government before the government converts the foreign funds into Chinese currency and then pays the exporter of the Chinese goods.

Over the past three decades, this system has enabled China to accumulate a staggering amount of dollars to add to its government reserves. At first, the inflow of dollars was relatively small because the trade between China and America was at a low level. For example, in 1980 China's foreign currency reserves amounted to only $2.5 billion in U.S. dollars. In the last three decades, however, the amount of foreign currency reserves held by the Chinese government has risen dramatically. In 2011 it stood at $3.2 *trillion*. This accumulation of foreign currency reserves amounts to an astonishing 127,940 percent increase over thirty years. When a foreign nation holds that much of another country's currency, the other country has a major cause for concern. When the time comes, know that China will use this advantage against the U.S. economy.

The State Administration of Foreign Exchange of the People's Republic of China (also known as SAFE) is a Chinese government investment organization that manages the country's trillions in foreign currency reserves. Over the past few years, the leaders of SAFE decided to invest most of China's foreign currency reserves in U.S. government securities, including currency notes, Treasury bills, and government bonds. As a result, some two-thirds of China's financial reserves are invested in U.S. securities. The next largest amount is held in investments tied to the Euro. Of course, virtually all of this money is earning next to nothing in today's market due to variable interest rates hovering near zero.

China's financial authorities would love to diversify the government's holdings into other vehicles tied to other nations' currencies, but the Chinese are essentially trapped by this huge investment in securities tied to the U.S. dollar. Very few other viable investment options are generating significant interest returns today. Even if the Chinese decided to do much more to diversify their holdings, if they were to begin rapidly selling off significant amounts of their enormous fund of U.S. government bonds, it would seriously depress the market value of those bonds.

China Is Purchasing Much of the World's Gold

China aspires to superpower status, and a leading factor in achieving political and economic power in the world involves a nation's being the source of the dominant currency used around the world. To achieve that, the Chinese want to back their currency with massive reserves of gold. The Chinese government thus is engaged in buying as much of the world's available gold supply as possible. In short, China wants to corner the global gold market. Financial historian Richard Russell observed that China wants the renminbi (the Chinese currency of which the yuan is the base unit) to be backed with a huge percentage of gold, thereby making the renminbi the world's best and most trusted currency.[1]

Several years ago Chinese authorities invested in U.S. stock markets but were almost wiped out when the market collapsed. Chinese economic authorities were held accountable and received harsh criticism from the Central Committee. Naturally, they are not eager to risk their reputation by investing again in a significant way in the U.S. stock market, which is why China's dollar reserves (invested in U.S. Treasury debt) keep piling up. Still wanting to diversify, the Chinese have found only one practical investment option available: gold.

Gold has been highly valued in China for thousands of years, together with silver, as an ultimate store of value. In 2011, China's purchase of gold reserves made it the largest buyer of gold in the world. Historically, India has been the world's major gold buyer. Traditionally the population of India has based its entire financial culture on gold. Meanwhile, silver had been the general store of value in China. But now, in China, gold has largely replaced silver.

Not only is China the world's leading buyer of gold, it also is by far the world's leading producer of gold. Every ounce of gold that is mined inside China—whether it is mined by the government or by foreign-owned mining companies—is required by law to be sold to the Chinese government.

The Chinese are accumulating such a staggering amount of gold that soon the government could be in position to back all its currency with government stores of gold. This would be a literal financial gold standard for the fastest-growing economy on earth. As befits a first-class world superpower, China's currency is on a path to become the first currency in the twenty-first century to be backed completely by gold. This is a big part of the reason why the Chinese government is trying to corner the global gold market.

If you doubt that the Chinese are attempting to corner the gold market, consider a diplomatic cable from the U.S. Embassy in Beijing to the U.S. State Department. (The contents of the cable were reported in 2011 by the website Wikileaks.) The embassy quoted a recent study regarding China's National Foreign Exchanges Administration: "China's gold reserves have recently increased. Currently, the majority of its gold reserves have been located in the U.S. and European countries. The U.S. and Europe have always suppressed the rising price of gold. They intend to weaken gold's function as an international reserve currency. They don't want to see other countries turning to gold reserves instead of the U.S. dollar or Euro. Therefore, suppressing the price of gold is very beneficial for the U.S. in maintaining the U.S. dollar's role as the international reserve currency. China's increased gold reserves will thus act as a model and lead other countries towards reserving more gold. Large gold reserves are also beneficial in promoting the internationalization of the RMB [China's currency]."[2]

The Chinese government's covert gold plan is proceeding on three fronts:

1. The Chinese government is engaged in massive, secretive purchases of gold bullion.

2. The Chinese government's investment agencies have invested staggering sums in the purchase of hidden stakes in a large number of foreign gold-mining firms.

3. The Chinese are behind ongoing changes being made to the international gold system.

Recent figures reveal that China produces more than three hundred tons of gold (9.6 million ounces) annually. China's production of gold is almost 50 percent greater than that of Australia, which is the world's second-largest producer. As mentioned previously, by law, all the gold mined in China must be sold to the Chinese government; none of it can be sold for export. In addition to government-owned gold mining, China buys massive amounts of gold from the International Monetary Fund (IMF) and other sources. China announced that its national gold holdings had risen by 75 percent due to purchases between 2003 and 2009. Since 2009, the Chinese have not announced their gold reserve totals, but there is evidence that China secretly continues to purchase massive amounts of gold outside the country.

As a result, China moved into the sixth position on the list of nations with the greatest foreign gold reserves. Still, even with such massive purchases, China's precious metal holdings accounted for less than 2 percent of the nation's foreign reserves. That's a tiny percentage when compared to the United States and Germany, which hold roughly 70 percent of their foreign reserves in gold bullion. The Reuters news agency suggested there was a sale of some 130 tons of gold to "unnamed" buyers, implying that China, at $3.2 trillion, was among the most likely candidates.[3]

Billionaire Eric Sprott is one of the most respected world authorities regarding investments in precious metals. He has purchased several hundred million dollars' worth of gold and silver in recent years for his firm, Sprott Resource Management. He reported that the China Investment Corporation acquired major stakes in some of the most productive mining companies in the world, including Anglogold Ashanti, Kinross Gold Corporation, Goldfields Ltd., and Teck Resources. The largest recent purchase was made by the Chinese government-owned Shandong Gold Group, the second-largest gold producer in China, which purchased Jaguar Mining for $785 million in cash.

Sprott said, "China's buying gold.... They see the gold price essentially go up every day. Well, it's not a difficult decision to say, 'Well, we should be buying gold and getting rid of dollars.'"[4]

The major concern related to China's gold-buying strategy is that it is rapidly turning China's national currency into a fully gold-backed currency. In the near future, this will make the U.S. dollar of much less importance in international trade and finance. As the financial newspaper *Barron's* reported, "China wants to establish the yuan as a [world] reserve currency that could someday challenge the almighty U.S. buck."[5]

China transformed its attitude toward the ownership of gold. For decades prior to 2002, Chinese citizens were forbidden to own gold bullion, but now the Chinese government encourages its people to purchase gold through thousands of gold stores and banks across China, where purchasers can choose from gold bars in four sizes.

Simon Black, a visitor to China, went to one of the gold stores and reported, "The government mints bars in sizes ranging from 5 grams to 1 kilogram. The gold prices are updated instantly...and the bars are all serialized and available at .9999 purity, the same as you would get from Switzerland."[6]

The Chinese are America's biggest creditors. Unfortunately, as America's debts compound at an ever-faster rate—and as the U.S. Treasury prints more and more currency to cover the escalating U.S. debt—America will suffer the greatest financial crisis in history. There is *no* way to avoid it.

America's Enemies Choose Their Point of Attack

Waging War on Our Country's Most Vulnerable Flank

Military strategists know the importance of protecting an army's flank. An enemy will hesitate to attack at the point where the opponent is strongest. Instead, the enemy will take advantage of an unguarded or weaker spot in the opponent's line of defense. This is just as true in sports as it is in war. Now, we see that this is true of the war being waged against the American Empire.

Few enemy nations would be foolish enough to attempt a frontal assault against the United States. After the terrorist attacks of September 11, 2001, America launched two wars against suspected complicit regimes. It took two presidential administrations to get it done, but eventually a team of U.S. Navy SEALs tracked down and killed Osama bin Laden, the country's number one enemy.

So a military assault against America would be far too costly to an enemy in armaments, troops, and the money it takes to finance an invasion. Any direct military engagement would be almost guaranteed to fail. So those who are committed to America's downfall sought a way to attack America's flank. They looked for a soft spot in America's national health. Where could an enemy probe a vital area and find weakness in order to gain a foothold and eventually leverage America's weakness in the enemy's favor?

International financiers and their allies found a weak spot: the U.S. economy.

For decades, America's leaders lacked the moral backbone to put an end to the looming disaster of deficit spending. It has been too easy to borrow money to finance government programs, many of them designed to attract a voting bloc and to reward campaign donors or home-district supporters. Overspending is financed by borrowing, with the underlying assumption that the national economy would continue to grow and employ increasing numbers of taxpayers who would pay not only for current (for them) government spending but also to make up the shortfalls in revenue from prior generations.

Simple reasoning, however, reveals that compounding debt year after year for forty or more years will dig a hole that is too deep to ever climb out of. But America's leaders have not been willing to face the truth, not to mention being unwilling to tell the voters the truth. Each administration creates problems for the next administration to clean up, and then the succeeding administration does the same thing. Congress is just as guilty of the same pattern.

We have reached the place where the national debt is so massive we will never recover from it. That is the hard fact that has handed America's enemies the weak spot they need. The American military is still strong. In fact, it is unmatched. But the economy is limping badly, and when you examine America for signs of strength and weakness, you have to conclude that the country is ripe for the picking. A stronger and more economically robust nation or political force could exploit our weakness to their advantage, destroying the American Empire in the process.

Attacking the Dollar

Why are the federal government and China conspiring to destroy the value of the dollar?

The official U.S. national debt in 2012 exceeded $15.6 trillion. This figure is nearly three times the combined debt owed by the most in-debted nations of the European Union. But to arrive at the actual fig-ure, we need to add in all the nation's debts plus the unfunded liabilities that Washington owes. When we add this up, it amounts to an almost unthinkable $145 trillion! This is nearly *ten* times higher than the oft-mentioned official national debt figure.

Not only is the true extent of the national debt vastly underreported, neither is it put into perspective relative to the nation's economy overall. A $145 trillion debt exceeds by nearly ten times the total value of all goods and services produced annually by the U.S. economy, usually stated as gross domestic product (GDP). Imagine that you earned $50,000 every year and that you owed credit card and other loan debt of $500,000, with none of that debt offset by personal assets. You would be so deep in a financial hole that you'd be bankrupt!

It is no different for the federal government. That $145 trillion debt is far more than the U.S. government can ever hope to pay back.

This brings us to the sobering solution that is the only remedy that remains. The government's only hope of not defaulting is to destroy the value of its own currency. By devaluing the dollar, the federal government can pay off its overwhelming debts and unfunded liabilities using highly inflated dollars worth only a fraction of their former value.

But when the Chinese yuan (the base unit of the renminbi currency) is strong in the face of a weak, inflated dollar, China is poised to buy up even more U.S. Treasury debt and thus protect their massive investment in America. In other words, China would protect its investment by helping the U.S. government avoid defaulting on its obligations. (No nation wants to hold huge investments in another nation that is headed toward bankruptcy.) In addition, a weakened U.S. dollar and a sturdy Chinese yuan would facilitate China's plan to buy enormous numbers of U.S. companies as well as American mining resources.

This situation will produce a massive win-win for both the U.S. government and China. In addition, the rising yuan would go a long way toward solving China's primary economic problem: a seriously rising rate of domestic inflation. As the Chinese yuan's buying power rises, inflation in China will decline dramatically.

More important for Beijing is that the yuan's expanding purchasing power fuels China's worldwide shopping spree. Chinese government agencies have been purchasing mining interests around the world that produce vast amounts of gold, copper, and other metals. China also is purchasing a staggering number of major Western businesses that are vital to China's future growth. China will be able to lock up even more of the world's limited but vital supply of oil, coal, steel, gold, copper, lumber, and other resources as well as take control of thousands of foreign companies.

Sadly, much of America's downfall is self-inflicted. Part of it is due to the unwillingness of our politicians to face the truth and take effective action years ago. Another part is America's leaders' willingness to conspire with the Chinese. The tragic news is that America, the country we love, is being sold to foreign interests by Washington's leaders.

How do you think voters would react if the president told the truth, "My fellow Americans, for many years we politicians in both parties have spent trillions of dollars that we don't have. Now, we simply can't pay our debts without borrowing huge sums from China. Beyond that, we will have to create new money out of thin air through the policy decisions of the Federal Reserve. The only way to avoid outright financial default is to destroy the value of our money in order to repay the nation's enormous debt with cheaper, inflated dollars. Unfortunately, this will mean your cost of living will double and then double again, and most of you will be reduced to poverty."

No president who wants to stay in office would ever say anything close to that. Instead, they rationalize and offer justifications that are palatable to voters who want to believe that the nation is in no immediate danger. It seems no one has the moral courage to face the hard facts and then do something to solve the problem.

Larry Elliott, economics editor of the *Guardian* newspaper in the United Kingdom, wrote, "The economic powerhouse of the 20th century emerged stronger from the Depression. But faced with cultural decay, structural weaknesses and reliance on finance, can the US do it again?"[1] I think not. The decline of America's economic, political, and, very soon, military power has reached such an advanced stage that all who want to understand our world must acknowledge that America's place in global trade, innovation, and military leadership is quickly diminishing.

Normally, I am an optimist, but I must admit that the overwhelming evidence points to an inescapable economic collapse. In this book, I describe the oncoming disaster with nothing but sadness. The nation's massive debt, however, leads me to this dismal conclusion.[2]

Increasing Demands on the World's Resources

In Mark Steyn's well-documented book *After America,* the commentator analyzes the decline of the economic and military power of the United States. He suggests that the historical core of Western civilization, as embodied in Western Europe, has lost so much vitality that it now is on a deathwatch. He further suggests that America is the only Western nation that could potentially carry the torch in the absence of Western European vitality. Steyn warns that America is very quickly following the European Union into a perpetual and severe decline. He calls for America's national leadership to awaken quickly and respond decisively, before it will be too late to turn things around. What we would be facing at that point would be the beginning of a new world in a dangerous, post-American superpower era.[3]

I would add that, sadly, America has failed to act, and we are certainly headed into the era of new world leadership. The West has lost its right to continue to lead the world.

Adding to the weakness of the United States is the rapid economic growth of a large number of developing nations. As more nations become industrialized, and as the energy needs of these developing nations increases, there is a far greater demand on the world's existing resources.

The surging economies of India, China, South Africa, and other countries now compete with the former powers from the West for the planet's natural resources. The basic economic law of supply and demand means that as more nations become industrialized and more nations consume more raw materials, the cost of these essential resources will rise. Availability will likewise decline. We have seen this already in China's shifts on export policy regarding the sale and export of rare earth elements (REEs).

Nations that formerly were large importers of goods from the West are now major manufacturers and producers of goods themselves. These developments, taken together, mean that the American Empire will face more and more shortages of vital commodities. As these materials become more expensive and harder to import, the economy and the military will suffer.

According to a 2010 commodities report titled "The Last Five Minutes," a major mining company estimated that the markets in mature developed countries consumed the following commodities:

- 59.6 percent of the world's copper
- 64.7 percent of the world's nickel
- 73 percent of the world's iron ore
- 62 percent of the world's metallurgical coal

This estimate of consumed commodities does not include the recently industrialized economies of Brazil, China, India, Malaysia, Mexico, South Africa, and Turkey.[4]

Helping to fuel America's industrial and technological ascendancy were bountiful and easily accessible mineral discoveries around the world, providing raw materials for manufacturing and developing new products and technologies. But since 2002 there have been no significant discoveries of previously untapped mineral deposits. This is true in spite of an expense of more than $22 billion in mineral exploration during the last decade. A resource analyst at Market Oracle declared that the last world-class mineral find was more than fifteen years ago.

Since 1850 we have mined, refined, processed, and consumed massive amounts of the easy-to-obtain minerals. Now we are forced to extract mineral deposits in smaller and smaller amounts, needing to remove them from larger and larger quantities of rock. The ore grades now available for the major mined metals are dropping in quality. This phenomenon requires modern mines to process larger amounts of raw ore to acquire much smaller amounts of vital minerals. Market Oracle's research shows that since large-scale mining began in the 1850s:

- Gold ore grades have dropped more than 91 percent
- Silver ore grades have dropped 91 percent
- Copper ore grades have declined 87.5 percent
- Lead ore grades are down by more than 75 percent
- Zinc ore grades have deteriorated by more than 50 percent[5]

Rare Earth Elements

The manufacture of many vital, high-technology products relies on fifteen rare earth elements (REE). Most of the world's deposits of these rare earth metals are found in only a few places on the planet, with China being a major source, along with a recent discovery in Greenland. The United States once was largely self-sufficient in these critical materials, but over the past decade American industry has become almost totally dependent upon imported REEs. While China is home to approximately 35 percent of the world's known reserves of REEs, that nation's mines produce about 90 percent of the supply that is used annually in North America and Europe.

A new very large REE deposit discovered at Mountain Pass, California, enlarged the known U.S. REE reserves to some 13 million tons, but it would take years to extract them, according to the first detailed report on the country's supply.[6] These REEs include fifteen rare metals:

Lanthanum
Terbium
Cerium
Dysprosium
Praseodymium
Neodymium
Erbium
Promethium
Thulium
Samarium
Ytterbium
Europium
Lutetium
Gadolinium
Yttrium

The diverse nuclear, metallurgical, chemical, catalytic, electrical, magnetic, and optical properties of the essential REEs have led industries to use them in an enormous variety of applications, including lighter flints and glass polishing applications as well as high-tech phosphors, lasers, magnets, batteries, and magnetic refrigeration. In addition, REEs are used in futuristic applications such as high-temperature superconductivity and the vital transport of hydrogen for a post-hydrocarbon economy. These difficult-to-find and difficult-to-pronounce rare earth metals are essential to the production of hybrid cars, surveillance satellites, superconducting magnets, camera lenses, and mercury-vapor light sources.

The demand for REEs is expected to exceed global production by 40,000 metric tons per year during the next decade. According to Robert Vance of the Nuclear Energy Agency, the global production of uranium, for example, reached its historic peak in 1980.

The world's demand for silver has exceeded the amount of silver mined annually for the last decade. One recent mining industry estimate concluded there are two decades' worth of silver left in the world's mines, based on the current demand.

Exacerbating the problems we face with diminishing sources of essential resources is the rapidly rising cost of extracting minerals and oil. This multiplies the prices charged for these resources.

The economic ratio known as energy return on investment (EROI) refers to the amount of energy it takes to extract a given amount of energy developed from oil. The United States was tapping huge, conventional underground oil fields with small, cheap derricks during the 1930s. At that time one hundred barrels of oil could be extracted by using the energy equivalent of one barrel. That means that during the Great Depression, American oil companies were producing crude oil at an EROI ratio of 100:1. While companies are now able to extract oil by drilling up to three or four miles beneath the seabed, accessing the massive oil sands of Western Canada, and with the promise of enormous reserves of oil shale, the development of such unconventional sources drives the EROI ratio closer to 11:1. It now takes the equivalent of one barrel of oil energy to bring eleven barrels to the surface.

Where the U.S. Economy Stands

Instead of leading the nation to courageously embrace a very difficult time of significantly reduced government programs and spending, the president and the Congress have decided to "solve" the problem by devaluing the dollar. This move will have grave consequences, but at the outset they can enact such measures without having to tell the voting public what really is going on. The deliberate destruction of the U.S. dollar will invite China to buy up U.S. industry, technology, and raw materials and also devastate the lifestyle of most Americans. It will drain the savings and pensions of people who have trusted the government to make good on its promises since the 1930s.

Our income, savings, investments, and retirements are being sacrificed on the altar of political expediency. This insult to national pride and patriotism will be painful, but the personal toll will be excruciating.

The steep drop in the value of the dollar will be catastrophic for everyone who earns, saves, or invests in any instrument based on U.S. dollars. The cost of living will skyrocket as well. The price of food, electricity, gasoline, and just about everything else will go through the roof. It stands to reason that a devalued dollar will no longer purchase a dollar's worth of goods or services. Prices will increase, and a dollar will more accurately be referred to as a fraction of a dollar.

Many Americans, particularly those living on fixed incomes, will be forced to choose between buying medicine, paying rent, or buying food. Homelessness, hunger, and hopelessness will become everyday realities for millions of Americans. Many who believed in the American Dream, who worked and saved, expecting to enjoy a secure retirement, will find their dreams and plans destroyed. The American public has played by the rules, but unfortunately their government has ignored the rules and broken trust with the people in order to serve the interests of the political elite and international financiers.

Why Are International Financiers Leading the Charge Against America?

It is difficult for most Americans to imagine why wealthy international financiers would want to cripple history's most successful, most prosperous economy. You might assume that the very wealthy have an intense desire to amass more wealth, and as a result they would do all they could to protect the U.S. economy. There is a clear logic that leads to that conclusion, but the facts before us lead to the opposite conclusion.

In the previous chapters we looked at how America has denied the founding principles that built the nation into history's most powerful empire. The loss not only of the founders' vision but also the bedrock principles upon which they built this nation have far-reaching consequences. A free people cannot remain free unless the rule of law is honored and defended. A free society cannot function when the federal government continues to usurp the rightful powers of the states and individual citizens. The gradual expansion of federal power at the expense of the states and individual Americans has brought us to the precipice where the United States now teeters.

Careful research into the decline and coming fall of the American Empire shows that those who are pulling the strings include both domestic and foreign political forces. They stand to gain a great advantage if they succeed in destroying the United States as a world power. So we need to ask the core question, Who would profit most from the fall of

America? If we can answer that question, we will take the first important step toward identifying the powerbrokers who operate outside the visible structures of government, military, diplomacy, and finance.

Tracing the Diabolical Trail

Let's begin this discussion by asking who would come out the winner in a political-military power shift away from the United States and in favor of some other world power. If global power shifted to Europe, China, or elsewhere, who would stand to gain the most?

This is how the international forces that support socialism are bringing an end to the American Empire. The U.S. armed forces are far superior in strength and technology to all other nations. This is comparable to the vast power of the Roman Empire in the days of Jesus Christ and the centuries that followed. The United States has built thirty-eight military bases around the world, primarily air and naval bases for long-range bombers and in support of the awesome naval forces that protect America's national interests around the globe. This preponderance of military power is similar to the dominance of Great Britain's naval forces and its well-trained army around the globe at the height of the British Empire's military supremacy in 1898. Such military domination, however, comes with tremendous economic cost, and over several decades it is difficult for any nation to sustain such a constant drain on its economy.

This was a lesson learned by the British Empire a century ago. It is the same lesson that is being taught today as the American Empire begins to face the hard truths that it can no longer afford to be the world's policeman. Similar to the British Empire in the years leading up to World War I, the leaders of the American Empire are beginning to realize that the nation's resources (economic, financial, military, and political) are not sufficient to meet the rising challenges from so many potential challengers.

The Military Decline of the United States

The war in Afghanistan is the longest armed conflict the United States has ever been involved in. Along with the Afghanistan and the Iraq wars, America is overextended in its longstanding role as global policeman. Not only do extended overseas wars deplete military readiness, but they significantly drain the U.S. economy by diverting massive wealth from the domestic front to an overseas war front. Money spent on supplies, military personnel, weapons systems, and so forth do not stimulate the U.S. economy, even when the goal of the war is honorable. Finally, after America's decades as the military defender of Europe, the Persian Gulf, and Asia, the proverbial chickens are coming home to roost.

Much of the blame behind the economic devastation of the American Empire can be laid at the feet of the Obama administration. While the nation was waging wars in Afghanistan and Iraq and the Great Recession was humbling the American economy, President Obama injected $1 trillion into a so-called domestic stimulus plan. The failed economic stimulus was devastating in two ways. First, it failed to accomplish its stated objective, namely, to revive the U.S. economy. Second, it multiplied the challenges facing the already strained federal budget, pushing it far beyond the breaking point. By inflating the national debt and deepening the national deficit, the Obama administration effectively negated America's economic options for years to come.

In January 2011 the Obama administration announced that the

U.S. military must become leaner while still maintaining its superiority. In a press conference at the Pentagon, the president revealed a far-reaching defense review that required a reduction in military forces of up to 100,000 troops. The president noted that the tide of war was receding in Iraq (after nine years) and that plans were being made to wind down U.S. military activities in Afghanistan. Therefore America must focus on renewing its economic power, and he chose the defense budget as the monetary whipping boy. The president's strategy calls for reductions in the Pentagon's expenditures by at least $450 billion over a decade.

In addition to cutting defense spending, President Obama is working to reduce America's nuclear defenses. The Newsmax organization reported that the president had undertaken an initiative that would weaken U.S. nuclear defenses and reduce them to the level of the nuclear defense shield of the 1950s. The existing treaty that set limits on nuclear arms, however, allows the United States to maintain a much larger nuclear arsenal. Meanwhile, China, Russia, and North Korea are not dismantling their nuclear forces to help balance the nuclear defenses among the nuclear powers.

The Obama administration is considering an overwhelming reduction of approximately 80 percent of U.S.-deployed nuclear weapons. These planned reduction options would be a historic, politically dangerous, and militarily dangerous disarmament step.

If President Obama chooses to unilaterally and somewhat secretly reduce U.S. nuclear strategic defenses to a level of only 300 deployed strategic nuclear missiles, this action would reduce U.S. defenses back to the levels of the 1950s. U.S. nuclear numbers peaked at above 12,000 in the late 1980s and only were reduced below 5,000 in 2003.

The United States is already on a well-planned bilateral negotiated treaty to reduce its nuclear strategic defenses to 1,550 deployed strategic nuclear warheads by 2018, as required by the New START nuclear treaty. As of September 1, 2011 the United States had 1,790 warheads, and Russia had 1,566, according to treaty-mandated reports published by each party.[7]

From Private Sector to National Emergency

The systemic financial problems that have impacted untold numbers of banks and companies across America have filtered to Washington and affected the U.S. Treasury. The problems of business eventually affect the federal government, and from there they filter down to you, your family, and all Americans who desire to protect their savings and their way of life.

The next phase in the inflationary crisis is approaching. The economic crisis will threaten most people's lifelong plans to accumulate sufficient wealth to finance their retirement. The savings of millions of Americans will be wiped out in the years ahead unless individuals respond now and in an informed way. This disaster will threaten to transform your business's fortunes and your life's work in ways that cannot be imagined now.

It is far too late to change the downward spiral of the nation's economy. Remember the analogy of having a $500,000 debt and no assets to use as collateral against that obligation? While the nation will descend into economic decline and chaos, it is not too late for individuals to take action to save their family's assets and accumulated wealth. The approaching crisis will change virtually everything that we associate with the American way of life, such as where you vacation, where you can send your children or grandchildren to school, the way you protect your family and home.

The Coming Implosion
of the U.S. Economy

Fed chairman Ben Bernanke has signaled that the Federal Reserve will keep interest rates near zero until late 2014, which is one and a half years later than he had promised previously. By the end of 2014 the U.S. government will have operated with near-zero interest rates for six consecutive years. An extended zero-percent interest rate is advantageous to the Treasury Department as the government continues to finance annual interest charges on the national debt of nearly $16 trillion.[8]

Eric Sprott, the founder of Sprott Asset Management, stated, "In 2008, when the Fed first introduced zero-percent interest rates, everyone thought it was a great policy. Four years later, however, and we're finally beginning to appreciate the complete destruction it has wreaked on savers. Just look at the horror show that exists in the pension industry today: According to Credit Suisse, of the 341 companies in the S&P 500 index with defined benefit pension plans, 97 percent are underfunded today."[9]

Let's not forget the enormous shortfalls regarding public sector pensions, which are outright frightening. In Europe, the total unfunded state pension obligations are estimated to amount to $39 trillion, which is approximately five times greater than Europe's combined gross debt.[10]

In the United States, unfunded pension obligations increased by $2.9 trillion in 2011. If the United States acknowledged these astonishing costs in its deficit calculations, the official 2011 fiscal deficit would have risen from the reported $1.3 trillion to $4.2 trillion. In long hand, that's an annual deficit of $4,200,000,000,000 in only one year.[11]

What are the other long-term effects of the Federal Reserve's actions?

What are the unintended consequences of keeping interest rates low in order to help the government manage the interest it owes on its debt? What are the repercussions of the excessive printing of money year after year? What are the dangers of excessive interventions by the Federal Reserve?

To begin to answer these questions, let's look at the European Union and the European banks whose liquidity was salvaged through the actions of the European Central Bank (ECB). The first observation is that without *continued* central bank support, interbank liquidity could cease to exist in a year or two. Consider the implications of the ECB's long-term refinancing operation (LTRO) program, a loan program designed to save the banks of the European Union. Participation in the program was voluntary, so each of the 523 banks that participated is admitting up front that they have a serious liquidity problem. This raises the question, How will these banks confidently lend money to one another again? If you are the head of a participating LTRO bank, because your bank has insufficient assets in relation to its liabilities, how can you trust any other LTRO banks that took advantage of the same program?

The LTRO program is potentially dangerous. It could prolong and even deepen the liquidity problem faced by Europe's banks. If the EU banks start to rely too heavily on loans from the central bank, the ECB may find itself inadvertently attached forever to the broken EU banking system.

The second unintended consequence is the serious impact that monetary interventions have had on the non-G6 countries' perception of Western solvency. If you're a foreign lender to the United States, Great Britain, Europe, or Japan, what is to prevent you from reassessing the stability and creditworthiness of those nations? Why would foreign lenders continue to pump money into the G-6 nations when the basis of these national economies, as a going concern, rests in their governments' ability to print more currency, injecting more cash into circulation? To take the matter a bit further, what happens when the rest of the non-G6 world starts to question the solvency and reliability of the G-6 central banks? What entity exists to bail out the financial system if the market moves against either the Federal Reserve or the ECB?

In 2008 and 2009, the G-6 nations' banks lost credibility when they required massive bailouts by their respective governments. In 2010 and 2011, many national governments (most notably those in Europe) lost their credibility and required massive bailouts by their respective central banks. However, there is no safety net, no lender of last resort for the European central banks themselves. In light of this, the International Monetary Fund (IMF) sought ways to raise an additional $600 billion as a security buffer.

The non-G6 world is not blind to the efforts of the Federal Reserve System and the ECB. When the Fed openly targets a 2 percent inflation rate, foreign lenders know that means they will lose, at a minimum, at least 2 percent of the purchasing power on their U.S. loans every year. It therefore should not surprise anyone to see those lenders chose alternative investments that show a greater potential to protect their wealth in the long term.[12]

This could well explain why China reduced its U.S. Treasury exposure by $32 billion in December 2011. This is also why China, which produced 360 tons of gold internally in just one year, imported an additional 428 tons of gold in 2011, up from 119 tons in 2010.[13]

The Looming Government Debt Disaster

When the Federal National Mortgage Association (known as Fannie Mae) and the Federal Home Loan Mortgage Corporation (known as Freddie Mac), the U.S. government guarantors of a huge percentage of the residential mortgages issued throughout America in the last few years, collapsed in 2008, the U.S. government chose to simply guarantee all of their outstanding mortgage debt. Unfortunately, since 2008 these government-backed companies have recorded hundreds of billions of additional losses, which were also passed along to the government. Remarkably, Freddie Mac and Fannie Mac are still operating, but the enormous costs associated with these mortgage guarantee programs are now accumulating in the U.S. Treasury. These mortgage losses and other private obligations have increased the accumulated debt to nearly $16 trillion.

The difficulty, of course, is that, prior to this currency and debt crisis, the federal government already was deeply in debt. With each commitment to absorb additional financial liabilities, America sank further and further into debt. America is approaching a time when the federal government can no longer afford to pay even the interest that is owed on its debt.

According to conservative calculations provided by the Congressional Budget Office (CBO), a debt default by the U.S. government would be inevitable were it not for one anomaly: the federal government can create money out of nothing. The U.S. government is the only debtor nation in the world that can legally print U.S. dollars. As a result, the federal government cannot go bankrupt in the ordinary sense of the word.

When things get too tight, the government can simply print more dollars to cover its bad debts. Since March 2009, the U.S. Treasury has been doing just that to keep the government afloat.

The dollar is still the world's reserve currency. America is the only country on earth that does not have to pay for its imports from other nations in a foreign currency, because the U.S. dollar forms the basis of the world's financial system. Banks around the world hold U.S. dollars in reserve against their loans.

Steps to Take Now

The most important aspect of the present monetary crisis is not what is hastening the crisis but what you can do to protect yourself, your business, and your family. Many will rightfully blame government officials for their misery. Others will blame Wall Street and the greed of the nation's bankers. My desire is to convince you that a full economic meltdown is imminent and that you need to act now to avoid the worst effects of that disaster.

Those who understand the reasons for the economic collapse and who take a few practical steps, which I will outline in the next chapter, will be able to avoid the worst of the financial fallout. You can protect your wealth and take action to increase your prosperity even as the American Empire fades into near obscurity.

America will suffer the greatest financial crisis in the nation's history. There is no way to avoid this disaster. However, those who are aware of what is coming can position themselves to benefit financially if they act quickly and appropriately.

How to Protect Your Family from the Looming Economic Collapse

Now Is the Time to Make Your Move

We are about to witness the certain collapse of the American Empire. This will have far-reaching effects on the rest of the world, because the fall of the world's unrivaled superpower will leave a tremendous power vacuum. Which nation or national leader will come forward in an attempt to replace the United States on the world scene?

Students of prophecy know the answer. With the American Empire rendered powerless by economic forces, which will in turn drastically reduce its military force, a new world power will emerge. The new superpower will be one that is the opposite of the United States, which has fought for freedom and defended liberty around the world. Soon the Antichrist will take the world stage, consolidating his political and economic power and extending the reach of his satanic regime. It is difficult for us to imagine the impact of this shift in power from America—founded on the truth of God—to the Antichrist, chosen and put in a place of world domination by Satan.

It's easy to think that since the Antichrist will rule the revived Roman Empire, the influence of his evil policies will affect only Europe and parts of Asia, the Middle East, and North Africa. But the Antichrist will be a world dictator, and no one on earth will escape the reach of his evil rule. No individual and no institution will be untouched.

As we discussed in the previous chapters, America soon will be devastated by a combination of unsustainable debt, competition from China, the decades-long plotting of international financiers, and the misguided cooperation of the top leaders in our federal government. The financial collapse of the American Empire will accelerate as our stifling national debt leads to bank failures, feeds rising inflation, and shakes investor confidence in American businesses and finance. No longer is the threat out there in the distant future. Already, even before we see any devastation take place, these things are attacking your family's security and financial well-being. It is up to you to act now to safeguard your future and to protect your family.

The question that you face—and the struggle that soon will confront every person reading this book—is this: Will you do all that is necessary to protect yourself and your family? While there is no guarantee that any of us will emerge from the impending crisis completely unharmed, you can take steps to mitigate the damage. You will be in a much better position if you take protective action now, compared to those who doubt the severity of the threat and who will put off doing anything about it. People who ignore this warning will dismiss my analysis of the world situation and the rapid decline of the American Empire.

When the colonists were making the decision to declare their independence from England, they knew they stood to lose everything if the British army were to prevail. But if the colonists won, they would have their freedom and the opportunity of self-rule and guaranteed liberty. In 1776 the threat was great, but the opportunity was even greater.

Today, Americans face another daunting threat. But this time it is not about taking a stand against the tyranny of the mother country. It is about reading the signs and seeing how close we are to the end of the empire that the founders birthed. The global chess pieces have been put into position to deliver the game-ending checkmate against America. This is not mere speculation. Our nation has gone far beyond the point where the tide can be reversed.

If you lost your home in the financial devastation of the current housing crisis, you might have thought that was as bad as things could get. If you contributed to a retirement fund for decades and suddenly the investments that were feeding that fund dried up so that your savings disappeared, you might think things cannot get any worse. If you have lost a job and now are underemployed or part of the long-term unemployed, you might feel that the economy has hit bottom and things can only start looking up.

I sympathize with you if any or all of these financial reversals have touched you and your family. Forces that are beyond the control of American's citizens have robbed us of our earning power, our savings, our prudent preparation for retirement, and the equity we were building in our homes. I do not want to discourage you, and I do not say this for shock value, but the simple truth is that the coming crisis is the most dangerous earthly threat facing you and your family. America's coming downfall from global superpower status to a greatly weakened, isolated nation far removed from the power center of the world will play havoc with your finances.

The nation's economy cannot be saved, but it is not too late to take remedial action to save your family's wealth and put in place the necessary safeguards so you can pursue future prosperity. This crisis will impact your savings accounts, your investments, and your retirement plans. The coming debt and inflationary crisis will change everything concerning your way of life.

Think about the practical, everyday issues you soon will be facing. The price of commodities such as milk, bread, and gasoline will soar. Most of your friends will not know what to do when their bank's doors close and their credit cards are no longer accepted by merchants. When banks are locked and ATM machines no longer accept your debit card, how will you access the money you thought you had in your checking and savings accounts?

Gold has been a solid hedge against inflation and against encroaching government for decades, ever since the international socialist conspiracy began to enlist national leaders within the United States. But what will you do when you are no longer allowed to buy gold or other precious metals or even more stable foreign currencies? What will you and your neighbors do when U.S. Savings Bonds are no longer worth even face value, much less paying the interest you thought you had earned on the investment? If you receive government assistance in any form, including Social Security, what will you do when the government checks are worthless and federal benefits are no longer worth the empty government promises that were made to the public?

Our monetary system is about to collapse. The dollar, which for as long as any of us can remember has been the standard currency around the world, will be close to worthless. This will come about because the federal government will devalue the dollar in order to cover its unpayable national debt.

For twenty years I was a professional financial planner in Canada, specializing in investments and estate planning. For more than forty years I have spent countless hours in investment and financial research as a serious investor. I know what I'm talking about.

In the very near future, you will not be able to rely on conventional safeguards, such as Social Security, a company pension, or other traditional retirement investments. These funds already are limiting and decreasing their promised payouts, and some have failed completely, becoming insolvent. So do not factor into your financial plan the retirement benefits you might have been counting on. We cannot save our nation's prosperity, but we can defend our right to secure a financial future for ourselves and those we love.

A Checklist for Financial Survival

Here are six steps you can take that will give you a good start toward protecting your assets and safeguarding your family's finances against the worst of what is to come with America's economic collapse. Bear in mind that some of these steps may not be options for you, depending on the laws and financial regulations that may apply in your locality.

Step 1: Prepare your financial defenses

All levels of government—federal, state, and local—will be forced to continually cut spending, step by step, as the economic crisis unfolds. Government spending reductions will go far beyond the minimal cuts we have seen up to now. So the first step is to determine how you will survive independent of any government assistance. You will need a plan for prospering on your own, without help from Social Security, Medicare, unemployment compensation, or any other government program.

Step 2: Make certain your bank is safe

One of the most important steps is to ensure that you won't lose your liquid assets due to a bank closure or failure. To prevent your savings from being lost in a bank closing, in the failure of a retirement fund, or in the reversal of certain equity investments, you need to make sure your liquid assets are in strong, reliable financial institutions. The Weiss Ratings service is the nation's leading provider of reliable independent ratings on more than sixteen thousand banks and credit unions. In 2010 and 2011, forty-nine relatively large banks and thrifts with assets of $1 billion or more failed. Weiss Ratings issued an advance warning on each of them before disaster struck.

Check out the rating of your financial institution by searching the Weiss Ratings " 'X' List Report: America's Weakest and Strongest Banks," www.uscentury.com/LinkClick.aspx?fileticket=0sajSG5Bu0c%3 D&tabid=6315. Weiss also examines and rates insurance companies. You can go to www.weissratings.com and search for the institutions you are concerned about. You will find for each the total assets and the direction its rating is headed. (For a fee, you can request detailed reports.) If your bank is rated as weak, immediately transfer your deposits to a strong bank in your area.

Step 3: Establish a solid wall of privacy regarding your finances

No level of government (federal, state, county, or local) will be your friend as the financial crisis unfolds. Remember, they all are hurting for money, and that need will only become more urgent. Governments at every level will become more desperate to generate revenue in any way they can. When considering the safest places to invest your assets, keep in mind that any bank transaction greater than ten thousand dollars must be reported to the U.S. Treasury. Further, any cash transaction that exceeds ten thousand dollars (for example, a purchase of jewelry or an automobile) must also be reported to the U.S. Treasury.

It is in your best interest to keep your financial affairs private, shielded from the prying eyes of government. You will not want any government representative to know more about your financial standing than is absolutely necessary. So shield your transactions by avoiding compulsory reporting. For example, if you have more than ten thousand dollars in cash to deposit, and you have researched stable banks and credit unions, rather than deposit the entire amount in one institution, break it into smaller amounts and deposit them in two or more banks. Further, if you are buying a high-ticket item such as an automobile, jewelry, boat, or travel trailer, avoid paying for it with cash.

Step 4: Own history's greatest hedge against financial crises—gold and silver

In 1995 I started recommending that my readers invest in gold. Since that time, gold coins and bars have risen in value by 437 percent, from

$400 per ounce to $1,750+ as of this writing. An initial $10,000 investment in 1995 would be worth approximately $43,370 today. It is still not too late to invest in gold. While the price of gold fluctuates, since 2001, when the price of gold bullion stood at $253 per ounce, its value has risen to $1,750 per ounce, an impressive 692 percent increase in a little more than ten years. You would be hard pressed to find any other investment vehicle that comes close to equaling the performance of gold and silver in the last decades.

Silver prices have risen from a low of $8.60 per ounce in 2001 to $32.00 per ounce at the end of 2011, an increase of 372 percent in one decade. So in addition to bullion coins, you should invest in U.S. silver coins that were minted from the early part of the last century until the U.S. Mint ceased to mint them in 1965. Unlike silver bullion bars or bullion coins, you can buy old coins for close to the spot price of silver (approximately $3.00 per coin), thus avoiding the typical premiums of 20 percent or more that you would pay for newly minted coins. A bag of pre-1965 silver coins often can be purchased at melt value. Another benefit is that because the coins are legal tender, they are precertified, date-stamped with the year of manufacture, and thus do not have to be assayed to prove their value before you buy or sell them.

Gold prices, even with the rise in value over the last several years, are likely to continue rising for at least the next three or four years. In 2011 the investment demand for gold increased by 20 percent (equal to $80 billion in gold). Purchases of gold bullion bars (primarily by China, Switzerland, Germany, and Austria) increased by 36 percent in 2011.

The reasons for the rise in the price of gold include:

1. The bull market in gold continues because a large number of central banks (which prior to 2009 would sell gold from their

vaults on an annual basis) have been buying large amounts of gold. The ongoing euro zone financial crisis, which makes headlines almost every day, has created uncertainty over the continuing value of the euro. Intensifying the effects of these factors is continued anxiety over a possible military strike against Iran, which would be triggered by the United States or Israel. If an airstrike destroys Iran's nuclear facilities, Iran is likely to retaliate by means of an attempted blockade of the Strait of Hormuz in the Persian Gulf. Also possible would be expanded terrorist acts against the West, in particular against Israel and the United States.

2. Unrest in the Middle East is nothing new, but since the spring of 2011 civil unrest and, in some nations, regime change have created power vacuums that are being filled by opportunistic political and religious factions. The continued instability in that region has triggered an enormous demand for gold and silver as a hedge against weakening national currencies.

3. There is a huge flight of capital from wealthy Middle Eastern investors who are transferring large percentages of their wealth out of the Middle East, the United Kingdom, Europe, and the United States. They fear that if they leave their investments in these regions, their wealth could be confiscated or in some way used against them for purposes of taxation or other loss of value. So these investors, in large measure, are moving into gold.

4. To move wealth from Europe, America, and the Middle East, Middle Eastern investors are placing huge amounts of gold bullion into financial institutions in Asia. As one example of the ex-

plosion of investing in gold, the Commercial Industrial Bank of China (with eighteen thousand branches) offers its one-billion-plus Chinese customers access to gold-based savings accounts. Meanwhile, the Chinese central bank is importing and adding to its reserves between forty and sixty tons of gold bullion every month. China plans to introduce a gold-backed currency by 2017 as an alternative to the current use of U.S. dollars as the preferred world reserve currency.

5. The relentless rise in inflation is motivating many investors to place a much greater percentage of their wealth into gold and silver. Although the Obama administration has said the national inflation rate is less than 3 percent, if we use the inflation-measuring method advocated by Paul Volcker, chairman of the Federal Reserve in the 1980s, we would find that the true U.S. inflation rate exceeds 11 percent.

In addition to the manmade reasons for the increased demand for gold, there also is the issue of a decrease in the supply of gold. The amount of gold being mined globally in each year of the last decade declined between 4 and 7 percent.

Many analysts who study gold prices believe gold will rise to $2,000 or more per ounce during the next year. It's not a bad idea to consider investing in precious metals, especially gold. The price of gold bullion has risen at an impressive rate over the last decade, significantly outperforming international stock markets and most other investments in commodities. The price of silver bullion has grown just as significantly, although silver is seriously underpriced in comparison to the price of gold. (Historically, the ratio of long-term value between gold and silver has been 16:1. If silver was following this ratio, with gold at approximately $1,660 an ounce, silver bullion should be priced at approximately $104. However, silver prices are significantly lower than that).

As you consider investing in precious metals, an effective strategy is to buy gold exchange traded funds (EFTs), which are 100 percent backed by physical gold. Also worth considering is gold-mining resource stocks, many of which have outperformed the rise in the price of physical gold.

Step 5: Go for huge gains as the economic crisis unfolds

During an economic collapse, a powerful investment offense is often your best defense. Act now and act decisively. If you can build up substantial cash and other liquid-asset reserves and do it as aggressively as possible, you can ensure your family's financial security for years.

We are about to witness the greatest wealth transfer in history, which will affect every one of us. For those who do the necessary research to educate themselves about the financial strategies summarized in this chapter, the economic meltdown can become a time of unprecedented opportunity.

Step 6: Protect yourself now against the looming economic downturn trends

Generally, avoid investing in commercial or residential real estate, other than your own home. Real estate has not yet bottomed out, and you do not want to invest and then lose money as the market continues to nosedive.

In addition, anyone who invests in real estate runs the risk of losing money due to higher inflation, rising mortgage rates, and higher rates of unemployment. This combination of factors will prove to be devastating for nonprofessional investors in the real estate market.

Difficult economic times call for difficult personal choices. In my opinion, and speaking strictly from a financial standpoint, I would advise you to consider selling your residence while there is a market for it. Rent a home until the crisis is over.

If you are committed to staying in your home and you have an adjustable-rate mortgage (ARM), immediately refinance your mortgage and switch from an ARM to the longest-period fixed-rate loan available. Do this immediately.

If you have decided to remain in your home and you are paying on a fixed-rate mortgage, do not pay down your mortgage ahead of the agreed-upon amortization schedule. With significantly higher inflation in the near future, you will soon be repaying the principle on your mortgage using much weaker dollars. This means you are getting the higher value of dollars from years ago but repaying that amount in dollars that will be worth far less. With growing inflation, the payments you make each year will cost you less and less in terms of the real value of the dollars.

By choosing not to pay down your mortgage more quickly, this could free up extra money. Put that money into shrewd investments or pay down other higher-interest debts, such as car loans or credit card balances.

Now is the time to reassess your retirement savings. Social Security will not provide a comfortable retirement income. In fact, the benefits under Social Security might be close to nil. Millions of Americans will find that they will have to work many years beyond age sixty-five to supplement their retirement savings.

The financial health of the Social Security system is highly uncertain due to the huge number of Baby Boomers that will retire in the next twenty years. Back in 1950 every recipient of Social Security was supported by the financial contributions of sixteen American workers. Contrast that with the current situation. The U.S. Bureau of Labor Statistics reveals that 1.75 active workers now support the Social Security benefits being paid to every recipient. The low ratio of contributors to beneficiaries (1.75:1) makes the Social Security system unsustainable.

Consider investing in foreign currencies, including Canadian dollars, Swiss francs, and Norwegian krones. To invest in foreign currencies, consider buying exchange-traded funds that benefit from strong major foreign currencies. To realize a good return on such investments, hold them as a long-term investment.

Additional Ways to Guard Your Financial Health

With the federal government taking steps to prevent you from making your own financial decisions, you need to act quickly and wisely. One step in this process is to convert your life savings into a currency that the government cannot control.

The U.S. insurance industry has a little-known provision that may allow you to access up to $250,000 from existing, unneeded life insurance coverage. Explore this $250,000 loophole, which might prove a godsend for anyone who requires extra retirement money.

Here is how it works where it is allowed. If you have a life insurance policy and your dependents will not need the death benefits upon your death, it's possible that you can sell part or all of the death benefits and receive as much as $250,000. You could then move the money into retirement savings. Some investors are willing to bid to acquire your death benefit, depending on your age. While insurance companies seldom discuss this option, it is legal. Older persons who own a life insurance policy they no longer need can sell part or all of the policy's death benefit through a specialized insurance broker. You can use the proceeds to augment your retirement funds.

The *Wall Street Journal* reported, "Few people know they have the option to sell their policies.... The growing life-settlements industry allows older people who no longer need or can afford a life-insurance policy to sell it to investors, who receive the [full] death benefit upon the insured's demise."[1]

Threats to retirement savings and healthcare

Dr. David Eifrig, a respected financial and investment advisor, has devoted himself to researching little-known methods to protect your assets from government threats. His approach is detailed in his column *Retirement Millionaire.*

It is important to commit to doing more research than ever before, especially since the federal government has begun enforcing little-known laws that could take a much bigger bite out of your assets. The provisions of the Capp's Law represent a significant threat to your hard-earned wealth and could adversely affect your retirement income, your family's healthcare, and even your ability to travel and purchase gold. You need to understand these laws so you can take the necessary steps to protect yourself and your family.

In a video posted by the *Daily Crux,* Eifrig describes these onerous laws as something that "reshapes one-sixth of the U.S. economy."[2] The restrictive laws are buried in thousands of pages of economic stimulus bills. They are referred to as Capp's Law because U.S. Representative Lois Capp (D-CA) voted for virtually every one of the provisions.

In 2011 the federal government began enforcing provisions of the law, with additional provisions set to take effect in 2013 and 2014. One of these 2013 provisions allows the government to seize a reported 4 percent in additional taxes from all investment income. This will reduce the return on investment for Americans who receive annuity benefits or who benefit from capital gains, dividends, interest, royalties, and rents.

Provision 5-I was enacted in February 2009 when Congress passed the first stimulus bill, which provided almost $800 billion for city, state, and federal government projects. Provision 5-I grants authority to the Federal Reserve to take funds from 401(k)s and other retirement vehicles over the next ten years. Disturbingly, the law does not state what amount can be seized, but well-informed insiders suggest it might be in the area of 4 percent.

Further, there is a little-known provision that allows the federal government to step in to make decisions for you regarding your healthcare. Washington could potentially control how much you can spend on cancer treatments or heart treatments as well as which types of drugs you would be allowed to use (even at your own cost).

The Open Threat of Provision 56-B

The Patriot Act was characterized as a necessary set of limitations on individual rights for the greater good of protecting the nation and assuring national security. But does the Patriot Act, on balance, deliver on the promise of protecting national security? The rules and regulations passed by Congress and signed by President George W. Bush following the terrorist attacks of September 11, 2001, were renewed under the Obama presidency. Provision 56-B gives the Department of Homeland Security the right to seize, without a warrant, an individual's bank accounts.

Federal authorities also can make periodic and unannounced visits to any bank in America, where they can open and inspect the contents of any safe-deposit boxes. Significantly, state authorities in California, Delaware, and Idaho have seized the contents of safe-deposit boxes under the pretext of determining if they were unclaimed property.

I mention these threats because they have been made completely legal by congressional legislation. If the federal government chooses to act on the most intrusive provisions of these laws, it could greatly damage your financial security. The best advice I can give is to do your homework, find reliable sources of information and advice, and then act quickly and decisively in advance of the fall of the American Empire.

America's Fall and the Rise
of the Antichrist

*How a Global Economic Meltdown Will Pave
the Way for Satan's Representative on Earth*

The worsening euro zone crisis, afflicting the economies of seventeen nations in the twenty-seven member European Union (EU),[1] demonstrates the international reach and unstoppable effects of the debt crisis. In late 2011 and early 2012 the crisis over the euro shook the foundations of what was thought to be a relatively stable European economy. The effects rippled around the world to threaten the global economy. The long-developing European Union crisis will have a profound impact on the economies of the United States and Canada, among the other leading nations of the world.

The economic crisis deepened as the European Central Bank (ECB) reconsidered its earlier policy of freely lending funds to Italy, Greece, and Spain. Investors were backing away from funding the region's major lenders. The latest attempt by the powerful Deutsche Bank AG of Germany to raise sufficient additional capital demonstrated the lack of enthusiasm among other European investors to respond to the many appeals for substantial EU funding.

This is not just a matter of risk aversion or individual nations looking out for their own interests. The tragic truth of the matter is that there is not enough available capital in Europe to finance the massive amounts of debt coming due in several EU-member countries. The irresponsible economic policies and practices of numerous EU nations have reached a critical point, threatening not just their own national economies but the health of the entire European Union. Financial analysts and the leaders of Germany and France believe dramatic changes must be implemented in the structure of the European Union if it is to survive as anything other than the proverbial sick man of the world economies.

Calls were issued for Greece, Italy, Spain, and Portugal to institute significant financial austerity programs in order to bring their government spending in line with their actual tax revenues. When those nations proved unwilling to act as speedily and decisively as the situation demanded, the nations that are the most committed to the goal of a European superstate began to demand substantial changes in the EU treaty. Economically stronger nations wanted mechanisms in place to force the weaker national economies to submit their annual budgets and taxation plans for approval by the European Union. Obviously, such a radical change in the relationships of the twenty-seven member states would require the members to surrender their autonomy in the areas of financial and tax policy.

Many top European politicians and economists agree that avoiding a complete collapse of the euro zone economies will require a more centralized European parliament. If that happens, the twenty-seven member nations will be forced to sacrifice significant portions of their independence and national sovereignty. This would result in a true united states of Europe, and that development would bring about the fulfillment of the biblical prophecies of Daniel 7 and Revelation 13. The prophets predicted that the nations that occupy the territories of the ancient Roman Empire will, in the last days before the return of Jesus Christ, unite in an unprecedented ten-nation superstate. This united, transnational entity would include both European and Mediterranean nations.

Daniel and John (in the book of Revelation) agree that, in the last days, a ten-nation empire will dominate first Europe and then the Middle Eastern nations of the Mediterranean. This new economic, political, and military empire will then dominate the rest of the European nations around the Mediterranean and the surrounding nations under the leadership of an eloquent global dictator, the Antichrist. He will be a brilliant economic genius (see Daniel 7), a world spiritual leader, and a military genius (see Revelation 13). Eventually this global dictator will rule the entire world. He will come to power with promises of peace (which will prove to be false) and then launch a series of military invasions until he subsequently imposes a total surveillance system around the world.

Joseph Farah's respected *G2 Bulletin* reported on the December 2011

EU crisis, stating that a well-informed European observer reported, "The old EU is finished. The 27-member bloc has never been as unpopular as it is today."[2]

The present EU treaty and the relationship between its twenty-seven member nations allows every EU nation to act independently regarding its own economy. The government of each member nation can set its own budgets and taxation levels. Individual EU national parliaments can dictate the limits of their EU participation, including spending, deficits, and taxation policy. A number of countries in southern Europe with fewer tax resources (and significantly fewer citizens paying their legally required taxes) are begging the more productive nations of northern Europe to assist them with economic bailouts.

Pouring good money after bad down a bottomless euro zone rabbit hole without requiring the southern EU nations to implement significant austerity measures is foolish, however. The northern European nations have already loaned hundreds of billions of dollars to Greece, Italy, Portugal, and Spain without demanding extensive budget cuts. Consequently, northern EU nations such as Germany (with a sustainable debt level of 81.5 percent of Germany's GDP, according to a 2011 estimate) and France (with its still healthy level of debt, 85.5 percent of GDP, based on a 2011 estimate) began to dictate financial terms to the southern EU countries, notably Greece, Italy, and Spain. Any further bailout money obtained by direct investments or through EU financial institutions, including the ECB and global institutions such as the International Monetary Fund (IMF), would depend on the southern EU nations' compliance with several belt-tightening measures.

Based on the level of interdependence within the European Union, it is deemed far too late to retreat to the time when the member nations exercised much more national sovereignty. The current economic and financial crisis has accelerated the pace of the European Union's advance toward a fully unified Europe that possesses greatly expanded economic powers and a shared government.

At an EU summit in Brussels in 2011, Germany and France proposed strict fiscal rules and financial penalties for euro zone member states that refused to adopt the necessary austerity measures. Germany and France proposed that the new rules should be written into the European Union's governing treaties, with the power of enforcement granted to EU federal institutions.

Great Britain objected to this proposal on the grounds that the European Union includes eleven members who are not part of the euro system. British prime minister David Cameron used his nation's veto against certain aspects of the proposed rescue package in order to ostensibly protect the financial interests of the city of London.

Many believe that what transpired at the Brussels summit was a watershed moment in the crisis. The Conservative Party in Britain concluded that empowering EU institutions to financially govern the euro zone could adversely impact Britain's independence and sovereignty. When France and Germany refused to negotiate, Cameron exercised Britain's veto. The result was that any move to create new financial rules for the euro zone nations would require treaty changes, which would be negotiated between willing member states. Interestingly, a poll revealed that 57 percent of British voters believed that Cameron was right to exercise their country's veto. Many British citizens desired a looser arrangement based around trade and the single EU market, without any requirement that member nations surrender increasing segments of their national sovereignty.

The United States of Europe

Many analysts of the European economic crisis argue that Europe is in the same circumstance that the thirteen American states faced prior to 1787, when the U.S. Constitution created a federal system for the new nation. Prior to 1787 the sovereign states formed a loose confederation that was governed by a congress. That legislative body was granted limited powers in foreign affairs plus the authority to borrow money, to deliver mail, and to handle affairs with the Native Americans. However, the Congress prior to 1787 did not have the legal power to collect any revenue from the individual states or to conscript troops until the thirteen states ratified the Constitution.

Charles Grant, a great believer in the European Union (EU) superstate, works for the Center for European Reform and believes that the economic crisis in the euro zone is exactly what is needed to motivate the leaders of the European Union to form a United States of Europe. He sees a need to transform the limited EU confederation of nations into a true democratically united Europe. If that happens, citizens of the member nations will be able to vote directly for the twenty-seven commissioners who formulate and enact virtually all of the region's vital policies, choose executives, and set and approve national budgets and tax levels. This makes the European Union a close parallel to the American voters who elect their representatives to the House of Representatives and the Senate.[3]

The Revived Roman Empire

More than five centuries before the birth of the Roman Empire, the Old Testament prophets predicted the rise of what would become the greatest empire the world had ever seen. Daniel proclaimed, "And the fourth kingdom [Rome] shall be strong as iron: forasmuch as iron breaketh in pieces and subdueth all things: and as iron that breaketh all these, shall it break in pieces and bruise" (Daniel 2:40). Rome was destined to conquer every nation that stood in its path. Yet when Daniel wrote his prophecy (approximately 580 BC), Rome was but a small Italian city-state of limited consequence. Without divine inspiration, no one could have possibly predicted that this tiny city-state would rise from obscurity to rule the world for more than one thousand years.

From 66 BC to 63 BC the powerful legions of the Roman general Pompey Magnus (Pompey the Great) conquered Syria and Judea, including the walled city of Jerusalem. At that time the Holy City had greater defensive walls than almost any other city in the world, including Damascus and Rome. During Pompey's siege of Jerusalem, the Roman legions slaughtered twelve thousand Judean soldiers in the final assault on the city and its temple mount. Jewish records suggest that the blood of the defenders of the temple were as high as a man's ankles in the battle for the Court of the Israelites. The Jews fought desperately against Pompey's troops to prevent the pagan soldiers from desecrating the Jews' most sacred holy place. After the conquest of the Jewish capital in 63 BC, the Roman legions established absolute rule over the population and the province of Judea.

Augustus Caesar ruled as emperor of the Roman Empire during the early life of Jesus Christ. During that period and into the following century, Rome's almost invincible legions expanded the empire to include the territories of what are now Egypt, Romania, Bulgaria, Hungary, Bosnia and Herzegovina, Croatia, and Serbia. Rome also dominated northern Europe, including the territories of what are now England,

Switzerland, Germany, northern France, and Belgium. No other empire had ever ruled so vast a geographical territory and great a population for such an extended period of time. Rome exercised military and political control over one hundred million subjects in an empire that extended more than one thousand miles, from the western coasts of Britain and Spain to the eastern edges of the deserts of Arabia.

The western portion of the empire fell in AD 476 to successive waves of Germanic invaders, which created a military power vacuum in Europe. The destruction of Rome's military, economic, and political leadership set the stage for the Dark Ages, characterized by virtually a thousand years of intellectual, religious, economic, and military decline.

The Eastern Roman Empire, however, based in Constantinople (now Istanbul, Turkey), continued to rule the eastern Mediterranean area as well as significant parts of Sicily, Italy, North Africa, and Spain. Remarkably, the leaders of the eastern empire (known as Byzantium) continued the Roman Empire's legacy for another thousand years until it fell to a Muslim conquest in AD 1453. After having survived many sieges, the city of Constantinople fell after the Muslims bribed a traitor in the city. The traitor opened the city's gates to the vast Muslim army. According to the Julian calendar, the siege of Constantinople began on Friday, April 6, 1453, and ended on May 29, 1453.

Most of the empires of history absorbed the culture, religious tradition, and technologies of the more advanced peoples they conquered. The Roman Empire was distinctive, however, in that it required its governors to eradicate the laws, religion, language, and society of every nation that was conquered. Rome replaced these conquered cultures with Roman laws and Roman culture. Many centuries have passed since Rome's unrivaled rule, yet the impact of Rome on subsequent Western societies and their history, customs, laws, and language remains unprecedented. After thousands of years, Europe, the Middle East, and even North America manifest numerous aspects of the ancient Roman forms of government, language, culture, and law.

Prophecies Regarding the Revived Roman Empire

The prophets Daniel and John prophesied that the Roman Empire would rise again to achieve world domination during the end of this age, the final seven years of the Tribulation, ending with the Battle of Armageddon. This period will usher in both the Antichrist and the long-awaited Messiah. This is happening today as the European Union sets the stage to become a dominant world empire.

In their Scriptures the ancient Jews saw a clear prophecy about a future satanic world ruler. This ruler, identified in the New Testament with the title Antichrist, will appear on the world scene to lead the revived Roman Empire. This new empire will become the unrivaled world power.

Philo of Alexandria was a respected first-century Jewish writer in Egypt. He wrote that the Antichrist would arise to oppress Israel during the last days, which would occur during the final generation before the return of the Messiah. In his book *On Rewards and Punishments,* the great biblical commentator declared, "For a man will come forth, says the prophecy [Numbers 24:7 in the Septuagint, the Greek translation of the Old Testament], who will go out and conduct a great war, and will overcome a great and powerful nation, as God Himself will assist His saints." This interpretation confirms a Jewish prophetic understanding that the rebirth of Israel must occur in the generation preceding the generation of the last days, when the Messiah will appear.

The book of Zerubbabel, an apocryphal volume written by an unknown Jewish author, includes a prophetic reference to the Antichrist using the name Armillus. This name is related to the ancient name Romulus, suggesting a strong connection with Rome. A number of early Targums (Jewish interpretive paraphrases of Old Testament passages) and commentaries on the books of the Old Testament also identified Daniel's "prince that shall come" (Daniel 9:26) as the future leader of the revived Roman Empire. Daniel prophesied, "The people of the prince that shall come shall destroy the city and the sanctuary; and the end thereof shall be with a flood, and unto the end of the war desolations are determined" (verse 26). Since the "people who shall come" who actually destroyed Jerusalem and the temple sanctuary in AD 70 were the Romans, many of the ancient Jewish sages taught that Israel's last great enemy would arise as a revived Roman Empire.

One of the greatest tragedies in Israel's history occurred during the Jews' final rebellion against Rome in AD 135, when the Roman emperor Hadrian slaughtered more than one and a half million Jewish soldiers and civilians. The victims of Hadrian's wrath had formed an army in an attempt to restore Israel's sovereignty under the leadership of the Jewish general Simeon Bar Kochba. The bloodshed occurred when Hadrian's generals defeated the armies of Bar Kochba, who had declared that he was the promised messiah.

This took place on the ninth day of the Hebrew month of Av (August), AD 135. This is the same date (the ninth day of Av) when Jerusalem and the temple were destroyed by the Babylonians in 587 BC. It also is worth noting that the ninth day of Av is the date that Rome's legions destroyed Jerusalem and the temple in AD 70.

In light of Hadrian's bloody defeat of Bar Kochba and the Jewish army, several rabbis have told me privately of their belief that the "spirit of Hadrian" will return in the last days. He will battle against Israel until he is finally defeated by the coming Messiah. Again, this Jewish belief clearly ties the coming Antichrist to a revived Roman Empire.

Interestingly, Jewish sages have debated for centuries about the precise time when the long-awaited Messiah will appear. Some rabbis have written that every Jew living in Israel needs to simultaneously repent at a single moment to motivate God to send the long-prophesied Redeemer. The ancient rabbis wrote in the Talmud about the time when the Messiah will appear: "All the predestined dates have passed and the matter [of Messiah's coming] depends only on repentance and good deeds.... Rabbi Joshua said: If they do not repent, will they not be redeemed? But the Holy One blessed be He, will set up a king over them, whose decrees shall be as cruel as Haman's whereby Israel shall engage in repentance, and he will then bring them back to the right path."[4]

This Jewish prophetic interpretation of a coming evil king suggests that God will use evil Gentile kings to bring Israel to repentance. The rabbis taught that the Gentile king of the last days will be "as cruel as Haman," the Persian enemy of the ancient Jews who tried, but failed, to destroy all the Jews throughout the 127 provinces of the Persian Empire. This was during the period when Ahasuerus (also known as Xerxes) ruled over the provinces from India to Ethiopia (see Esther 3–9). The rabbinic interpretation that cites Haman's cruelty parallels the Christian prophetic commentaries regarding Daniel's prophecy that the Antichrist would rise to global power in the end times and would rule over Israel in order to motivate the Jews to repentance before God.

Previous Failed Attempts to Revive the Roman Empire

Daniel prophesied the revival of the Roman Empire in the days preceding the coming of the Messiah. Twenty-five centuries ago, the prophet wrote, "After this I saw in the night visions, and behold a fourth beast, dreadful and terrible, and strong exceedingly; and it had great iron teeth: it devoured and brake in pieces, and stamped the residue with the feet of it: and it was diverse from all the beasts that were before it; and it had ten horns. I considered the horns, and, behold, there came up among them another little horn, before whom there were three of the first horns plucked up by the roots: and, behold, in this horn were eyes like the eyes of man, and a mouth speaking great things" (Daniel 7:7–8).

Once again the ancient Roman Empire will rise to take its dominant place on the stage of world history. Daniel also predicted that the restoration of the Roman Empire would appear in an unprecedented form: a superstate confederacy composed of ten nations. The member nations of the European Union currently occupy the territory of the Roman Empire—Western Europe and the nations surrounding the Mediterranean Sea. A powerful dictator, the "little horn" in Daniel's prophecy, will arise to rule this new empire by defeating three of the ten leading confederate nations and then seize power over all ten nations and their subsidiaries (see Daniel 7).

From the time of the disintegration of the Western Roman Empire in AD 476 until the end of the Second World War, the peoples and nations of Europe, the Middle East, and northern Africa have experienced centuries of violent military and political struggles. Warfare dominated European affairs for almost fifteen centuries. During this period, a number of political, religious, and military leaders dreamed of recreating the Roman Empire. The first serious attempt was led by Charlemagne (Charles the Great) in AD 800. His failed effort to re-create the Roman Empire was followed by numerous attempts over the following centuries led by various Roman Catholic pontiffs.

Despite the efforts of England's Henry II to create a European empire by uniting the territories of England and France in the late 1100s, his heirs abandoned the quest after his death. Almost six centuries later, during the societal chaos that followed the French Revolution, Napoleon Bonaparte seized power in 1800 to pursue a scheme to re-create a vast European empire similar to that of ancient Rome. Napoleon had ambitions to include the Middle East in his empire, thus he invaded Egypt. But despite his military victories, Napoleon's opponents in Europe joined together with the growing military force of England to form an alliance that finally defeated the French at the battle of Waterloo in Belgium in 1815, and Napoleon's dreams of European conquest ended.

More than a century later, during the 1930s, the Italian fascist dictator Benito Mussolini tried and failed to re-create the Roman Empire. In the same decade, German chancellor Adolf Hitler created a political, economic, and military colossus that threatened all of Europe, the Soviet Union, and ultimately the entire world. Hitler's plans to conquer the world launched the Second World War. He dreamed that his Third Reich (literally, Third Empire) would endure for a thousand years as a revival of the ancient glories of Rome. Tragically, more than sixty million people died as a result of Hitler's ambition.

The Rise of the Antichrist

The prophet Daniel's miraculous ability to interpret dreams and prophetic visions brought him to the attention of Nebuchadnezzar, the king of Babylon, in 587 BC. The Babylonian king had a strange dream about a huge human image composed of four metals: gold, silver, bronze, and iron. Daniel explained that this image symbolized the future courses of four successive world empires, from the time of Daniel (during the sixth century BC) until the end times of this age. The prophet interpreted the dreams and then prophesied that four major Gentile empires would, in sequence, rule the known world. This would begin with the Babylonian Empire and proceed through the centuries with the Greek Empire of Alexander the Great, the world empire of the Medes and the Persians, then the Roman Empire. Sixteen centuries would pass until the Roman Empire would be revived during the generation of the Second Coming of Christ.

In his dream, Nebuchadnezzar saw a metallic image of a man who had "feet and toes, part of potters' clay, and part of iron" (Daniel 2:41). Daniel's interpretation pointed out that "the kingdom shall be divided; but there shall be in it of the strength of the iron, forasmuch as thou sawest the iron mixed with miry clay" (verse 41). Later, Daniel described a parallel prophetic vision of an image of a beast that "had ten horns," representing the ten nations that would arise in the last days within the territory of the Roman Empire (see Daniel 7:7). The two prophetic visions suggest that the fourth Gentile empire will arise in the form of ten European Union nations as well as the nations allied to the European Union in the territory surrounding the Mediterranean Sea. Daniel's description of "ten toes" and "ten horns" suggests the future course of the growing European Union, which may be the embryonic political and military power base of the coming Antichrist's world government. Daniel's prophetic time line indicates that the revived Roman Empire will rise to global power during the years leading up to the Second Coming of Christ.

Later in his life, Daniel received another prophetic vision from God that depicted the final destiny of the revived Roman Empire: "After this I saw in the night visions, and behold a fourth beast, dreadful and terrible, and strong exceedingly; and it had great iron teeth: it devoured and brake in pieces, and stamped the residue with the feet of it: and it was diverse from all the beasts that were before it; and it had ten horns. I considered the horns, and, behold, there came up among them another little horn, before whom there were three of the first horns plucked up by the roots" (Daniel 7:7–8).

Daniel's vision suggests that ten nations will join together in the end-times confederacy. In the last days, a dynamic new leader of Western Europe (the "little horn," symbolizing the Antichrist) will take advantage of a crisis in Europe and will seize control of three of the ten European nations through peace treaties and the use of overwhelming military force. The remaining seven nations will then submit to the power of the Antichrist and accept his dictatorial rule. The Antichrist's conquest of the three European nations will be his first military success on a long road to supreme world power. The Antichrist will rule for an unknown number of years, but the Scriptures declare that in his position as head of the revived Roman Empire, he will then guarantee a security treaty, or "confirm the covenant," with Israel for a period of seven years (see Daniel 9:27). Daniel foretold the Antichrist's seven-year covenant with Israel in his prophecy: "And he shall confirm the covenant with many for one week: and in the midst of the week he shall cause the sacrifice and the oblation to cease, and for the overspreading of abominations he shall make it desolate, even until the consummation, and that determined shall be poured upon the desolate" (verse 27).

The Antichrist will wield absolute political and military power over every nation on earth, and he will exercise his satanic power over the Tribulation saints who find faith in Christ during this time of brutal persecution. After the bodily resurrection (the Rapture) of the dead saints (whose spirits died before the Tribulation and are now in heaven) as well as the simultaneous glorification of all living Christians, millions of Jews and Gentiles who are left on earth will examine the Scriptures in a search for answers about why hundreds of millions of Christians have disappeared without a trace. Millions from every race around the world eventually will reject the propaganda of the world dictator and will place their faith in God as a result of their study of the Bible and the message of the "two witnesses" and the 144,000 Jewish witnesses (see Revelation 7:14–17; 11:3–12). These new converts to faith in Jesus will come from every nation. They are the millions of Tribulation saints described in the book of Revelation[5]: "After this I beheld, and, lo, a great multitude, which no man could number, of all nations, and kindreds, and people, and tongues, stood before the throne, and before the Lamb, clothed with white robes, and palms in their hands.... And one of the elders answered, saying unto me, What are these which are arrayed in white robes?... And he said to me, These are they which came out of great tribulation, and have washed their robes, and made them white in the blood of the Lamb" (Revelation 7:9, 13–14).

John's prophecies indicate that the Antichrist's domination over the

Tribulation saints will continue throughout the entire seven-year Tribulation treaty period. The Antichrist will defile the rebuilt temple in Jerusalem at the midpoint of the seven-year Tribulation. From that point to the time of his final destruction and death in the Battle of Armageddon at Jesus Christ's return will be three and a half years (see Daniel 7:25 and Revelation 13:5–7).

Political Plans for Global Government

The North Atlantic Treaty Organization (NATO) was established in 1948 by the victorious Western Allies of World War II. They created the trans-Atlantic alliance to ensure a common defense of the Western European democracies against a growing military threat from the Soviet Union and the Warsaw Pact. Much has happened since the adoption of the NATO mutual-defense pact. The process of creating a European superstate began in 1957 with the Treaty of Rome and the negotiations that established the European Common Market, officially known then as the European Economic Community (EEC).

The Treaty of Rome set the stage for the European Union to become an economic, political, and military colossus. In 1979, Europe held the first election for the European Parliament, creating history's first directly elected, multinational, superstate assembly. Without realizing it, the people of Western Europe took the first step toward fulfilling Daniel's prophecy of the coming ten-nation superstate.[6]

The French intellectual Jean Monnet, the spiritual father of the idea of a United States of Europe, revealed the ultimate political objective of the new superstate: "Once a common market interest has been created,

then political union will come naturally."[7] In 1992, the Treaty on European Union set the rules for a single EU currency as well as laid the framework for a unified foreign policy, security policy, and closer cooperation in justice and domestic affairs among the member nations.

The European Union is gradually accepting additional member states, now consisting of twenty-seven nations. Norway and Switzerland earlier had declined to membership but are now reconsidering. The success of the integration of the individual European national economies, together with the growing forces of globalization, have convinced most Europeans that national independence may be a political luxury they can no longer afford. Many of the poverty-stricken nations of Eastern Europe, including Bulgaria and Romania, have qualified as members. They saw EU membership as a promise of economic prosperity and the only hope to defend their weak democratic governments from communists still hoping to be restored to power.

The first superstate currency: the euro

Dr. Hans Tietmeyer, president of the German Federal Bank (also known as the Bundesbank, or central bank), declared, "A European currency will lead to member nations transferring their sovereignty over financial and wage policy as well as in monetary affairs."[8] Europeans are realizing that joining in the EU confederacy could mean the practical abolishment of their laws and customs and even control over their nation's political future. The European Union's introduction of the euro currency in 1999 was a significant step toward creating the world's first superstate economy, an effective common market, and the elimination of trade barriers between the member states. Euro banknotes and coins came into public circulation in 2002.[9]

The totalitarianism of the European Union

In the past, corporations and governments in various European nations were impacted by significant currency exchange costs. The adoption of the euro paved the way for fully integrated, Europe-wide tax systems as well as a common fiscal and monetary policy. Fifteen centuries after the fall of the Roman Empire, the economically and militarily powerful nations of Europe are systematically transforming themselves into virtual provinces of the world's first superstate, the basis of the coming global superpower described in the prophecies of Daniel and John.

The signs of the coming world government go far beyond a shared currency and trade arrangements that favor EU-member nations over the rest of the world. Laws and trade regulations from the European Union already impinge on national laws, customs, and more.

In a superstate system such as the European Union, unelected bureaucrats tend to issue regulations without any accountability or the authority that comes from being elected by the people. In addition, the typical democratic remedy to correct bad decisions is unlikely to work because the EU regulators are not subject to political pressure from members of the European Parliament. As a result, the ability to correct bad EU decisions is virtually nonexistent. Despite the trappings of democracy, the directly elected European Parliament cannot affect major laws, taxes, or the choice of executives, but it now has the ability to at least vote on and amend two-thirds of the EU's laws.[10]

The pattern displayed by international organizations is that real political power is exercised secretly by key members of an elite group, operating from behind locked doors. History suggests that meaningful, representative government can function only at the local or national level. Once in the arena of international politics, democratic systems are replaced by sophisticated bargaining and trade-offs negotiated behind the scenes.

The political and economic power centered in the European Union's European Commission is a preview of how ultimate power will be exercised in the coming world government. Pressure to achieve faster and greater centralization of government in the EU territory will be felt due to the heightening euro zone crisis.

European economic sickness

Today, throughout the seventeen-nation euro zone, unemployment is at historic levels. Eurostat, the European Union's statistical office, reports that 16.3 million people are out of work in the euro trading area. Figures for Spain reveal that 51.4 percent of citizens aged sixteen to twenty-four are without jobs. In Greece, the figure is 43 percent; in Italy, 28 percent. With European nations facing austerity measures for the foreseeable future, and the euro zone GDP as a whole predicted to shrink, the economic and unemployment outlook will continue to be bleak.[11]

Unquestionably, the scene is set for the arrival and rise to power of the Antichrist.

11

America After the Meltdown

Hardly Any Aspect of Your Everyday Life
Will Be Left Unchanged

A democratic form of government cannot remain strong without a national character that is moral and committed to God's principles. A strong and free nation also relies on the individual character and values of its government's leaders. Defending democracy requires continual vigilance and the willingness of citizens to sacrifice their personal advantages when necessary, together with responsible military policies and reasonable antiterrorism legislation. These fundamental values are under attack, and without these democratic values in place, democracy cannot stand.

It is easy to track the decline in faith and moral fortitude on the national level, which prevents our national leaders from defending democracy and democratic institutions in a way that is consistent with the U.S. Constitution. The Scriptures point out that among the twelve tribes of Israel, the tribe of Issachar was chosen by God to be blessed with the ability to know and understand the prophecies of God. In 1 Chronicles 12:32 the Lord promised Israel, "And of the children of Issachar, which were men that had understanding of the times, to know what Israel ought to do."

With strong national character—its citizens and its leaders—a nation can withstand daunting challenges. We know this to be true of America, because the United States has been governed by three succeeding forms of government and has grown and prospered under each.

First, the European immigrants who organized the original thirteen colonies were ruled by England. The British monarchy was unresponsive to the colonists' grievances. "Taxation without representation" was only one of the burning issues that turned the patriots against British rule.

Second, the government of the American colonies was transformed in 1776 with the signing of the Declaration of Independence. Armed insurrection followed, and the colonies were governed during this interim period by the Articles of Confederation.

Third, after the Revolutionary War, the Founding Fathers wrote the Constitution for the newly independent nation. This new document, which would replace the Articles of Confederation, was ratified in 1788 and has served the nation well since then. Even during the Civil War, from 1861 to 1865, when eleven states seceded from the Union and rejected the authority of the Constitution, the wisdom contained in this governing document continued to serve the nation well while a war was waged to restore the Union.

The Constitution has been amended over the years, but in recent years activist justices on the Supreme Court have chosen to enact laws by fiat, with little regard for legal precedent or the binding principles of the nation's founding document. There will come a time when America loses this form of government, and the transition will come in an attempt to avert another political crisis, as was last seen in 1861 with the first shot fired in the Civil War.

The twentieth-century battle over the Constitution has extended into the twenty-first century. Loose constructionists and strict constructionists continue to argue over the original intent of the framers and the legitimate application of that intent to modern governance. The issues are too numerous to discuss here, but one stands apart from the rest due to its potential to destroy the nation. In fact, there is abundant evidence that it already is doing its work to put an end to the American Republic.

The issue at hand is the supposedly impenetrable "wall of separation" between church and state. The United States should be based on religious tolerance, which includes the public recognition of its profound Christian heritage. The Protestant Christian principle of religious tolerance has served America well, and the outcome has been that this nation has welcomed many people of various religions. People have been drawn to America and have adopted it as their home. They brought their skills and talents to this land and have helped build history's greatest empire. Contrast that tradition of tolerance with what is experienced today—and throughout Islam's history—in a Muslim nation. While America encourages free thought and initiative, the Muslim world requires conformity of thought and practice.

Historical records and contemporary examples tell us that religious toleration is not a value that is held by most of those of the Islamic faith, and certainly not to those who live under the strict dictates of shari'ah law. Here is just one telling example. While Christian churches have survived in the Middle East for almost nineteen centuries, Islam is committed to eradicating them. The highest Muslim religious authority in Saudi Arabia, the Grand Mufti, Sheikh Abdul Aziz bin Abdullah, declared on March 16, 2012, that all churches in the Arabian Peninsula (dating back more than five centuries before Mohammed) must be destroyed. The statement naturally prompted anger and dismay from Christians throughout the Middle East. The Grand Mufti made the controversial statement in response to a question from a Kuwaiti NGO delegation called the Society of the Revival of Islamic Heritage. A Kuwaiti parliamentarian had called for a ban on the construction of new churches; however, the initiative has not yet been passed into law.

Here is the irony of religious tolerance in America. Tolerance is guaranteed in the Constitution, and it has helped immensely in building the American Empire. However, today in America, one religion is singled out to be silenced in the public square. That targeted religion is Christianity. The influence of Christianity on the nation's history and culture has been denied and effectively silenced in what once was the greatest nation on earth.

How the Imperial President Violated Your Conscience

There is no better evidence of this intolerance than the way President Obama thumbed his nose at the religious convictions, moral standards, and matters of personal conscience of tens of millions of Christians. Over the last few decades the federal government has introduced a large body of legislation that interferes unnecessarily with the lives of individual Americans and encroaches on the constitutional rights and powers of the states. The federal government cites its so-called power to regulate interstate commerce, using that argument to justify a wide range of restrictions and regulations. This interference reaches into almost every aspect of the economy.

It is a vast distortion of the interstate commerce clause to expand it into a carte-blanche justification for virtually every policy that some leaders within the federal government want to enact. This continual overstepping of the government's legitimate authority spelled the beginning of the end of the rule of constitutional law in America. Now the Constitution is virtually a dead letter. The founding document of this nation has been selectively reinterpreted and misinterpreted by the U.S. Supreme Court to the point that the Court has practically nullified the entire document.

President Obama's healthcare legislation, the Patient Protection and Affordable Care Act (also known as Obamacare), *requires* that every citizen purchase health insurance. This is a clear violation of the U.S. Constitution. The Obama administration claims that the federal government has the power to regulate interstate commerce and, by extension, that Washington has the power to take over healthcare for all citizens. But if you read the Constitution, you will see that the mention of "interstate commerce" occurs only in the preamble to the Constitution, in which the Founding Fathers explain why this document is necessary. The truth is that the regulation of interstate commerce is not an enumerated power granted to the federal government. Moreover, the Tenth Amendment states, "The powers not delegated to the United States by the Constitution, nor prohibited by it to the States, are reserved to the States respectively, or to the people." Since the Constitution does not give such powers to the federal government, President Obama's attempt to exercise this power is unconstitutional.

In March 2012 the U.S. Supreme Court heard arguments challenging and defending the healthcare law. A survey showed that as many as two-thirds of the American people wanted the law and the individual mandate (the requirement that every citizen carry health insurance) to be rejected by the High Court. The Supreme Court listened for five hours to the arguments of the attorneys representing the federal government and defending the law as well as those representing a number of state governments that had challenged the law. The legal question to be decided had to do with whether the Constitution's commerce clause has any limits. If the federal government can compel a private citizen, under threat of a federally imposed penalty, to engage in a private contract with a private entity (in this case, to buy health insurance), one must ask if there is anything the federal government cannot compel a citizen to do? If this law were to be declared constitutional by the highest court in the land, would there be no end to the overreaching of the federal government?

On June 28, 2012, the Court rendered a controversial verdict on the Affordable Care Act. Shockingly, Chief Justice John Roberts penned the majority opinion that ruled the individual mandate was constitutional, but he did so in a way that surprised everyone. Although the main argument had been that the government had the authority to make such a mandate under the commerce clause to compel citizens to purchase health insurance, the majority opinion asserted that this was not justifiable under the commerce clause. Instead, Roberts interpreted the mandate to be a tax, and Congress has the unlimited authority to tax citizens who do not purchase insurance. Never before, however, has a penalty or tax been levied on the people of this country for inactivity.

The sad truth is that the Obama administration has undertaken and succeeded in the most significant attack on the U.S. Constitution and its guarantees of liberty for all. Worse, the Supreme Court, which is entrusted with the responsibility to protect the Constitution and safeguard Americans from government abuse, found a way to allow this grievous attack on freedom to go forward.

Prior to the announcement of the Court's decision, Charles Krauthammer, in an article titled "The days of reckoning for Obamacare" in Canada's *National Post,* pointed out that the healthcare law was on the political landscape as a result of the Congressional Budget Office's revised cost estimates, the pending Supreme Court ruling, and the issuance of a compulsory contraception mandate. The annual gross costs of the Affordable Care Act for the years following 2021 are more than a quarter of a trillion dollars. Thus, the president has introduced a huge entitlement program in a nation that already is drowning in $16 trillion of debt.[1]

"A lot of employers are going to drop their health insurance coverage to dump people on government-run exchanges to get them off their neck," Philip Klein, senior editorial writer for the *Washington Examiner,* told CBN News.[2]

Not only is the Affordable Care Act more expensive than originally proposed, the costs for this massive takeover of healthcare will significantly increase taxes on the middle class. After the Supreme Court ruled that the mandate was a tax, *Wall Street Journal* senior economics writer Stephen Moore explained who is going to bear most of the burden. "You remember the President's promise that when he was elected no one who makes under $200,000 a year would pay a dime more of taxes," he told Fox News, "we found that about three quarters of…whatever you want to call them—taxes, fines, penalties—about three quarters of those costs will fall on the backs of those who make less than $120,000 a year. It's a big punch in the stomach to middle-class families."[3]

Moreover, the Affordable Care Act will most likely not reduce insurance expenses but will rather lead to increased medical costs and insurance rates. Peter Suderman, senior editor at *Reason Magazine,* said, "The CBO says that this law is going to cost a trillion dollars in new spending. Is it going to bring down the cost of insurance? Well, it's going to subsidize the cost of private insurance, but as we know from the long history of health subsidies and other subsidies, when you subsidize something, what happens is that the market raises the price to account for those subsidies. And so I think it is at least very unlikely that ultimately this law helps contain the cost of insurance premiums, helps slow the growth of medical spending overall."[4]

Obamacare's Independent Payment Advisory Board

While most of the Affordable Care Act is objectionable to supporters of limited federal government, there is one part that is absolutely indefensible. Deep within the pages of the act is a description of the Independent Payment Advisory Board (IPAB), which has the power to oversee the Medicare budget. Essentially, this board can write its own laws. According to Peter Orszag, former director of the Office of Management and Budget (OMB) for the Obama administration, "President Obama fought hard for IPAB, over strong opposition from Congress, which saw the board as usurping its power. When IPAB starts up in 2014, it will comprise an independent panel of medical experts charged with devising changes to Medicare's payment system. In each year that Medicare's per capita costs exceed a certain threshold, IPAB will be responsible for making proposals to reduce this projected cost growth to the specified threshold. The policies will then take effect automatically unless Congress specifically passes legislation blocking them and the president signs that legislation. In other words, the default is that [IPAB's] policies…will take effect."[5]

How can it be that anyone would approve such a bold and anti-constitutional aspect of this law? The Affordable Care Act takes the legislative power out of the hands of Congress and places it with an unelected body that can decide how much Medicare should be cut and what services should be provided, all of which will affect the healthcare of millions of Americans. Not only do the IPAB's legislative proposals become law once they are written, the only way they can be overridden is if both houses of Congress *and* the president agree on a substitute proposal.

Unbelievably, this board will have powers well beyond Medicare. Diane Cohen, senior attorney at the Goldwater Institute, and Michael Cannon of the Cato Institute explain, "IPAB will have the power to ration or reorganize care even for those who are not enrolled in government programs. The Act grants IPAB the power to regulate non-federal health care programs and private health care and health insurance markets, so long as such action is 'related to the Medicare program,' 'improv[es] health care outcomes,' and serves IPAB's other stated goals."[6]

The Loss of State Sovereignty

America was created as a union of sovereign states, not a federated country with provinces such as exist in Canada. Political sovereignty resides in the fifty states, but they loan their fundamental political and legal powers to the national government. America is a federal republic, and the federal government's powers are derived from the states, and therefore those powers can be revoked. If the federal government goes too far in overstepping its constitutional powers, and the abuse becomes too severe, the states could take action.

This is why some commentators see the possibility of a future uprising within America. It would not be armed conflict, as was the Civil War. Instead, it would be the formulation of a viable legal mechanism by which a state or group of states could lawfully secede from the Union. The mechanism would require that the federal government, having abused its power to an extent that no longer can be tolerated, would be required by law to accommodate such a move. In this way, the sovereign states could exercise their rights and act against the growing totalitarianism in Washington DC.

This is the ultimate check and balance on the federal government, and it is the only way to ensure that citizens are never again forced to live under tyranny without legal and political recourse. No one wants another violent revolutionary conflict or internal civil war. In consideration of the rising national debt and the massive entitlement crisis that will bring the United States to the brink of economic collapse, Americans will need to create a new government that will live within its means and will abide by the Constitution's safeguards and requirements. It will be a small, unobtrusive federal government that no longer taxes citizens beyond what is reasonable.

The Coming Economic Catastrophe

America is facing a complete economic meltdown brought about by the reckless actions of the Federal Reserve as it continues to inflate the U.S. monetary system with trillions of dollars of new currency. This will bring on enormous inflationary pressure, driving up the cost of living and devaluing the assets of ordinary Americans.

The United States will not be completely destroyed by the coming economic catastrophe. The nation will survive the coming collapse, but the nation that will emerge from this catastrophic reversal will bear little resemblance to the global empire that was the America of the twentieth century.

As Christians, we have hope, and we know that our protection does not derive from a government but from God. There is reason to hope that America's economic collapse will produce a far less powerful nation that will return to the founding principles that served the fledgling nation well in the eighteenth century. The Articles of Confederation, in effect during the Revolutionary War, ensured limited representative government, a "rule of law; not of men," and the cooperative efforts of the sovereign states in coming together to fight for a united cause.

The crisis that is brewing will soon come to a head, and no institution of government will emerge from this untouched.

I am not a prophet, but reading the best and most reliable economic indicators and having followed the trajectory of America's politics, actions in the world, and its unsound economic policies for more than a quarter century, I can make credible, informed predictions. The current form of government that is characteristic of the American Empire will almost certainly fall. I do not make that statement with any level of satisfaction. I do not relish the destruction of history's only nation founded intentionally on God's truth. But I do have a grounded conviction that the American Empire will soon cease to exist. Keep in mind that this crisis does not mean America will no longer be a functioning nation.

America is a people, not a government. America is a union of fifty sovereign states, each with its own government, bound to its fellow states by history, language, culture, shared goals and values, and common experiences. The demise of the present form of the federal government will not break apart this union. The nation will most certainly be redefined, and in many ways the new America will bear little resemblance to what we know now as the United States.

I do not anticipate insurrection, but I foresee a significant upheaval in the laws that limit and determine how we are governed. Following the coming financial upheaval, it will probably require a constitutional convention to reinstate and clarify the founding principles that gave birth to the American Empire. Whether the current U.S. Constitution survives or is replaced by a new one, I do not know. The type of government America produces will of necessity reflect the fundamental constitutional rights that citizens demand.

The new America will adhere to the constitutional requirements that have long been lost in the current federal system. The new system will reflect the people's desire for limited representative government. Among the needed changes will be careful controls and limits on the federal government's ability to borrow funds beyond its ability to repay.

The best possible response to the coming crisis would be passage of a constitutional amendment that prohibits the federal government from spending more than current assets and federal tax revenues allow (save in time of war). This measure also would restrict the government from creating additional debt and printing excessive currency. If America can live within its tax-revenue limits, this would go a long way toward releasing all citizens from the burden of unsustainable government debts. A limit on future government borrowing would go a long way toward a true restoration of the Founding Fathers' dream of a limited republic.

The fundamental choice to live within its means would require a significant reduction of social programs to keep the federal budget in line with tax revenues. The decision by the Congress and a future president to either support or reject this restriction on the government's ability to borrow money to finance federal programs would, to a great extent, determine the future financial and geopolitical strength, posture, and influence of America after the collapse.

Unless politicians find the political and moral resolve to live within the nation's financial means, America will be destroyed financially.

Will future political leaders choose to require future governments to live within their means, or will they continue to borrow funds despite the fact that such practice leads to bankruptcy? It will require a hard decision by principled leaders to impose a realistic financial solution.

The incredible events that will take place in the coming months will cause many to question what lies ahead for the world. There is a growing fascination with the prophecies of the Bible regarding the events of the last days. The crisis that is about to come upon us provides a tremendous opportunity to share practical strategies of preparation as well as to share our faith in Jesus Christ, who is our ultimate security in an uncertain world. It is well to remember the words of the Bible: "Set thine house in order" (2 Kings 20:1).

Appendix A

The Clear Intent of the Founding Fathers

Secularists like to argue that a significant number of America's Founding Fathers were deists whose view of God and Scripture bore little similarity to the orthodox understandings and teachings of historic Christianity. This is not the place to argue that point, but this much is clear: even the handful of founders who might not have held in all ways to a fully orthodox faith were still men who took their cues from God and His written Word. It was not a situation, as secularists would have us believe, in which the founders discounted the value of the Scriptures and regarded God as a disengaged, impersonal deity.

To show the many ways in which the Founding Fathers gave God credit for laying the foundation of the new nation, I have collected a number of quotations from their writings and speeches. These quotes demonstrate the commitment these men had to seeking the guidance, help, and wisdom of God.

The Declaration of Independence

July 4, 1776

When in the course of human events, it becomes necessary for one people to dissolve the political bands which have connected them with another, and to assume among the powers of the earth the separate and equal station to which the laws of nature and of nature's God entitles them, a decent respect to the opinions of mankind requires that they should declare the causes which impel them to the separation.

We hold these truths to be self-evident, that all men are created equal, that they are endowed by their Creator with certain unalienable rights, that among these are life, liberty and the pursuit of happiness. That to secure these rights, governments are instituted among men, deriving their just powers from the consent of the governed.

And for the support of this Declaration, with a firm reliance on the protection of Divine Providence, we mutually pledge to each other our lives, our fortunes, and our sacred honor.

Thanksgiving Day Proclamation, 1789, by George Washington

By the President of the United States of America.

A Proclamation.

Whereas it is the duty of all nations to acknowledge the providence of Almighty God, to obey His will, to be grateful for His benefits, and humbly to implore His protection and favor; and whereas both Houses of Congress have, by their joint committee, requested me "to recommend to the people of the United States a day of public thanksgiving and prayer, to be observed by acknowledging with grateful hearts the many and signal favors of Almighty God, especially by affording them an opportunity peaceably to establish a form of government for their safety and happiness."

Now, therefore, I do recommend and assign Thursday, the 26th day of November next, to be devoted by the people of these States to the service of that great and glorious Being who is the beneficent author of all the good that was, that is, or that will be; that we may then all unite in rendering unto Him our sincere and humble thanks for His kind care and protection of the people of this country previous to their becoming a nation; for the signal and manifold mercies and the favorable interpositions of His providence in the course and conclusion of the late war; for the great degree of tranquility, union, and plenty which we have since enjoyed; for the peaceable and rational manner in which we have been enabled to establish constitutions of government for our safety and happiness, and particularly the national one now lately instituted; for the civil and religious liberty with which we are blessed, and the means we have of acquiring and diffusing useful knowledge; and, in general, for all the great and various favors which He has been pleased to confer upon us.

And also that we may then unite in most humbly offering our prayers and supplications to the great Lord and Ruler of Nations, and beseech Him to pardon our national and other transgressions; to enable us all, whether in public or private stations, to perform our several and relative duties properly and punctually; to render our National Government a blessing to all the people by constantly being a Government of wise, just, and constitutional laws, discreetly and faithfully executed and obeyed; to protect and guide all sovereigns and nations (especially such as have shown kindness to us), and to bless them with good governments, peace, and concord; to promote the knowledge and practice of true religion and virtue, and the increase of science among them and us; and, generally, to grant unto all mankind such a degree of temporal prosperity as He alone knows to be best.[1]

George Washington

The first president of the United States, George Washington, wrote a letter to the Baptist churches of Virginia regarding the importance of the First Amendment to the U.S. Constitution. Washington explained, "Every man…ought to be protected in worshipping the Deity according to the dictates of his own conscience."[2]

He explained to his Baptist readers that the First Amendment did not guarantee "a separation of church and state." Rather, the First Amendment guaranteed American citizens the freedom of religion and worship. It is clear from the writings of the Founding Fathers that the Constitution and the First Amendment were not designed to protect the government from the influence of religion but to protect religion from the federal government's interference.

In his first speech to Congress, Washington stated his view regarding the role of God in the providential birth of the American Republic: "No people can be bound to acknowledge and adore the Invisible Hand which conducts the affairs of men more than the people of the United

States. Every step by which they have advanced to the character of an independent nation seems to have been distinguished by some token of providential agency.... We ought to be no less persuaded that the propitious smiles of Heaven can never be expected on a nation that disregards the eternal rules of order and right, which Heaven itself has ordained."[3]

At the end of his presidency, Washington wrote the following in his farewell address: "Of all the dispositions and habits which lead to political prosperity, religion and morality are indispensable supports."[4]

Thomas Jefferson

Thomas Jefferson, the principal author of the Declaration of Independence (1776) and the third president of the United States (1801–1809), wrote about the spiritual basis of America. He noted that the United States was based upon God's provision: "Can the liberties of a nation be thought secure when we have removed their only firm basis, a conviction in the minds of the people that these liberties are of the gift of God? That they are not to be violated but with his wrath? Indeed, I tremble for my country when I reflect that God is just; that his justice cannot sleep for ever."[5]

Thomas Jefferson wrote to Dr. Benjamin Rush, "My views...are the result of a life of inquiry and reflection, and very different from the anti-Christian system imputed to me by those who know nothing of my opinions. To the corruptions of Christianity I am indeed opposed; but not to the genuine precepts of Jesus himself. I am a Christian, in the only sense he wished any one to be; sincerely attached to his doctrines in preference to all others."[6]

Jefferson also wrote, "Can the liberties of a nation be secure when we have removed the conviction that these liberties are the gift of God?"[7]

James Madison

James Madison, the fourth president of the United States (1809–1817), is considered the father of the Constitution. He wrote the following in 1778 to the General Assembly of the State of Virginia: "We have staked the whole future of American civilization, not upon the power of government, far from it. We've staked the future of all our political institutions upon our capacity…to sustain ourselves according to the Ten Commandments of God."[8]

John Quincy Adams

John Quincy Adams, the sixth U.S. president (1825–1829), was strongly influenced by the Word of God and possessed a strong personal faith in Jesus Christ. Adams later became the president of the American Bible Society and wrote the following to that organization: "The Bible carries with it the history of the creation, the fall and redemption of man, and discloses to him, in the infant born at Bethlehem, the legislator and savior of the world."[9]

Adams also wrote, "So great is my veneration for the Bible that the earlier my children begin to read it the more confident will be my hope that they will prove useful citizens of their country and respectable members of society."[10]

Benjamin Franklin

Benjamin Franklin was one of the greatest thinkers who helped develop the concepts behind the U.S. Constitution. He also was a signer of the Declaration of Independence. He cited a belief in God and His inspired Word in the creation and foundation of the new American Republic.

In Franklin's speech to the Constitutional Convention of 1787, he declared, "The longer I live, the more convincing proofs I see of this truth—that God governs in the affairs of men. And if a sparrow cannot fall to the ground without his notice, is it probable that an empire can rise without his aid? We have been assured, Sir, in the sacred writings, that 'except the Lord build the House they labour in vain that build it.' I firmly believe this; and I also believe that without his concurring aid we shall succeed in this political building no better than the Builders of Babel."[11]

John Adams

In a letter to Thomas Jefferson on June 28, 1813, former president John Adams (1797–1801) wrote, "The general principles on which the fathers achieved independence were…the general principles of Christianity.… I will avow that I then believed, and now believe, that those general principles of Christianity are as eternal and immutable as the existence and attributes of God; and that those principles of liberty are as unalterable as human nature."[12]

Adams wrote about the fundamental and essential importance of the Christian basis of the American Republic: "We have no government armed with power capable of contending with human passions unbridled by morality and religion.... Our Constitution was made only for a moral and religious people. It is wholly inadequate to the government of any other."[13]

Adams later asserted, "It is religion and morality alone which can establish the principles upon which freedom can securely stand. Religion and virtue are the only foundations...of republicanism and all free governments."[14]

Noah Webster

Noah Webster was a political writer, an editor, and a prolific author. Webster commented on the fundamental importance of Christianity to religious liberty in America. He wrote, "The religion which has introduced civil liberty is the religion of Christ and His apostles...to this we owe our free constitutions of government." Webster also stated, "The moral principles and precepts contained in the Scriptures ought to form the basis of all our civil constitutions and laws. All the miseries and evils which men suffer from, vice, crime, ambition, injustice, oppression, slavery, and war, proceed from their despising or neglecting the precepts contained in the Bible."[15]

John Jay

John Jay was the first chief justice of the U.S. Supreme Court. Jay wrote about the vital importance of the Word of God in the life of the American Republic: "Providence has given to our people the choice of their rulers, and it is their duty—as well as privilege and interest of our Christian nation—to select and prefer Christians for their rulers."[16]

Regarding the Bible, Jay wrote to his son, "The Bible is the best of all books, for it is the word of God and teaches us the way to be happy in this world and in the next. Continue therefore to read it and to regulate your life by its precepts."[17]

Appendix B

How America's Past Leaders Relied on God

It was not just the founders of the United States who relied on the Bible and expressed that reliance in official pronouncements as well as personal correspondence. In the decades and centuries following, presidents and other high government officials reaffirmed that stand again and again.

Andrew Jackson

President Andrew Jackson declared, "[The Bible] is the rock on which our republic rests."[1]

Abraham Lincoln

The beloved Abraham Lincoln wrote the following words regarding the overwhelming importance of the Word of God: "In regard to this Great Book [the Bible], I have but to say, it is the best gift God has given to man. All the good the Saviour gave to the world was communicated through this Book. But for it we could not know right from wrong. All things most desirable for man's welfare, here and hereafter, are to be found portrayed in it."[2]

In Lincoln's first inaugural address on March 4, 1861, he spoke about the profound importance of Christianity to the governing of this unique nation. Lincoln declared, "Intelligence, patriotism, Christianity, and a firm reliance on Him who has never yet forsaken this favored land, are still competent to adjust, in the best way, all our present difficulties."[3]

Later, discussing his personal study of the Word of God, Lincoln wrote, "I am profitably engaged in reading the Bible. Take all of this book upon reason that you can, and the balance by faith, and you will live and die a better man."[4]

A Remarkable Affirmation
by the U.S. Supreme Court

In an 1892 case being heard by the U.S. Supreme Court, the Court made a definite declaration of the Christian basis behind the fundamental laws and governmental institutions of America. The majority decision of the Court declared, "Our laws and our institutions must necessarily be based upon and embody the teachings of the Redeemer of mankind.

It is impossible that it should be otherwise; and in this sense and to this extent our civilization and our institutions are emphatically Christian.... This is a Christian nation."[5]

Calvin Coolidge

President Calvin Coolidge wrote about the spiritual and biblical basis of the United States: "They [the Founding Fathers] were intent upon establishing a Christian commonwealth in accordance to the principle of self-government. It has been said that God sifted the nations that He might send choice grain into the wilderness.... Who can fail to see it in the hand of destiny? Who can doubt that it has been guided by a Divine Providence?"[6]

Franklin D. Roosevelt

President Franklin D. Roosevelt acknowledged the centrality of belief in Christ and His doctrines to the foundation of this unique republic. "[The United States is] founded on the principles of Christianity."[7]

Harry S. Truman

President Harry S. Truman stepped into the awesome responsibility of replacing President Franklin Roosevelt before the end of the Second World War. He was very aware of the tremendous importance of the Word of God: "The fundamental basis of this Nation's law was given to Moses on the Mount. The fundamental basis of our Bill of Rights comes from the teachings which we get from Exodus and St. Matthew, from Isaiah and St. Paul."[8]

Dwight D. Eisenhower

Dwight D. Eisenhower, a general of the Second World War, was elected president of the United States in 1952. He wrote, "Without God, there could be no American form of government, nor an American way of life. Recognition of the Supreme Being is the first, the most basic, expression of Americanism. Thus, the founding fathers of America saw it, and thus with God's help, it will continue to be."[9]

Ronald W. Reagan

President Ronald Reagan had a deeply felt belief in Jesus Christ and His teachings. He said, "Of the many influences that have shaped the United States into a distinctive nation and people, none may be said to be more fundamental and enduring than the Bible."[10]

Appendix C

The High-Tech World of Future Warfare

While *One Nation, Under Attack* deals primarily with attacks on America by way of pushing the nation over the brink of bankruptcy, it is interesting to note that in addition, technology has been applied to ultramodern warfare techniques and weapons systems. It is very possible that a rogue nation, terrorist organization, or other entity could make use of developing technologies such as are described here.

Each of these weapons has a legitimate military application, but it also could be used by terrorists to inflict great damage. In the wrong hands, each has the potential to disrupt society, transportation, trade, banking, infrastructure, communications, and other systems that are critical to carrying out the nation's economic activities.

Direct-Energy Photon Weapons

Science fiction fans have enjoyed the television show *Star Trek,* which theorizes about space wars that take place in the twenty-third century. In addition to handheld phasers, the starship *Enterprise* fires photon torpedoes, which project balls of light energy across the vacuum of space. The idea that pulses of light energy could be focused and fired effectively at enemy vessels seems implausible to most of us. A major reason to question such a weapon is the tendency of acoustical or electromagnetic energy to disperse as it travels through space.

American and Russian researchers, however, have developed long-distance, directed-energy-beam weapons. The patent issued for the invention states, "The invention relates generally to transmission of pulses of energy, and more particularly to the propagation of localized pulses of electromagnetic or acoustic energy over long distances without divergence." The patent also describes the effect of the beamed energy as "electromagnetic missiles or bullets" capable of destroying virtually any targeted object at extreme distances.[1]

The "Voice of God" Weapon

The United States has created a weapon that can project a verbal or visual message from a great distance into the mind of an enemy combatant. Knowledgeable insiders suggest that the designated target will perceive the message as having a supernatural origin, as if it were coming from God. Imagine suicide bombers or terrorists on a mission suddenly hearing a voice in their head telling them to desist from their planned destruction.

Two technology companies, Holosonic Research Labs and American

Technology Corporation, developed their own versions of this sound-directing technology. There are reports that U.S. troops in Iraq and Afghanistan used a similar system to confuse and disorientate enemy combatants.[2]

A Thermobaric Rifle

After years of research aimed at increasing the power of handheld weapons issued to infantrymen, the Pentagon equipped soldiers in Iraq and Afghanistan with a thirty-three-inch-long weapon that vastly increases their firepower. According to an article in *Wired* magazine, the thermobaric bomb is "a fearsome explosive that sets fire to the air above its target, then sucks the oxygen out of [the atmosphere surrounding] anyone unfortunate enough to have lived through the initial blast." Thermobaric ammunition contains a computer chip that can be programmed so the charge explodes over the heads of enemy soldiers or terrorists hiding in buildings.[3]

The Silent Guardian Microwave Weapon

A high-tech weapon developed by Raytheon and known as the Silent Guardian, is the size of a large plasma television screen and can be mounted on the back of a Humvee. When energized, the Silent Guardian emits microwaves at a precise frequency, which stimulate human nerve endings. This can be done over a distance up to a half mile. The device emits a beam that penetrates the skin of the target to a depth of one sixty-fourth of an inch, thus the Silent Guardian does not cause visible or permanent injury to the target. Soldiers who volunteered to test the effects of the weapon were not able to resist it for longer than a second. They fled the target area due to the intense discomfort caused by the microwaves.[4]

Weapons Using Radio Frequencies

Some reports describe a sophisticated weapon that uses radio frequencies (RFs) to produce enough static electrical energy to destroy high-tech equipment such as computers. A new form of these weapons, transient electromagnetic devices (TEDs), could destroy the electronic infrastructure of societies, including government offices, financial institutions, aircraft, medical facilities, and electronic equipment. Unfortunately, these devices can be assembled using readily available electronic parts costing less than five hundred dollars. Electronic frequency weapons generate wide-band radio pulses in the nanosecond and picosecond range using megawatt power and gigahertz (microwave) frequencies. Directional radio-frequency antennas send radio pulses to attack specific targets. If terrorists were to use such a weapon, it could easily be disguised as a small satellite dish.[5]

It is possible to protect vital computer systems against RF attacks, but the cost is prohibitive except for the most vital government computer systems.

Camouflaged Electronic Devices

U.S. military technology includes electronic camouflage devices that alter the appearance of military vehicles, causing their surfaces to simulate or match the colors and textures of the immediate background. This camouflage technique makes a lightly armored vehicle virtually invisible to the naked eye from a distance. Sophisticated cameras record the physical elements in the immediate background—such as sand, earth, and vegetation—and then electronically projects these images onto the surface of a vehicle encountering enemy combatants. The enemy sees only what is behind the vehicle, allowing the vehicle to virtually disappear.[6]

Space-Based Weapons

The February 2012 issue of *Future Threats Monitor* details the United Kingdom's complacency over space superiority. The article discusses the national security issues concerning the potential of an enemy's use of space weapons against the Western nations, including the United Kingdom and the United States.

On February 22, 2012, the Defense Select Committee of the UK government released a report titled "Developing Threats: Electro-Magnetic Pulses (EMP)," which examined the military risks to all developed nations of the use of a space-based EMP weapon attack. The report warns that over the next decade existing space-launched vehicle technology could be utilized by nuclear-capable states to deliver a small nuclear warhead, either in a direct strike or an atmospheric detonation. The UK's Ministry of Defense reported that the attacker would utilize an improvised nuclear warhead that would be detonated at high altitude, possibly three hundred miles above a targeted nation. Use of such a space-based nuclear warhead would generate widespread damage from an electromagnetic pulse weapon.

In the 2009 report titled "Global Single Point Failure: The EMP Threat," the U.S. EMP Awareness Coordination Task Force (EMPACT) noted that some rogue states such as Iran and North Korea are aware of the potential destruction that can be caused by such an attack. Iran is reported to have conducted a test in the late 1990s to simulate a nuclear EMP strike.

A surprise EMP attack would instantly destroy all unshielded electrical equipment, including generators, leaving the targeted nation in the dark for an extended period. An EMP attack would destroy the communications infrastructure of an advanced nation, including the banking system, its stock market, virtually all transportation systems, and the pumping of fuel, among many, many other electricity-based systems. In short, a space-based EMP attack would throw back the targeted state to the technological capacity of the late nineteenth century.

NOTES

Introduction

1. Michael Ignatieff, "The Burden," *New York Times Magazine*, January 5, 2003, www.nytimes.com/2003/01/05/magazine /05EMPIRE.html?pagewanted=all.

2. The Lord does, however, refer to the global evangelism explosion, which is led by the church in North America during the last days.

Chapter 2

1. Demos.org, "The State of Young America: The Databook," November 2, 2011, www.demos.org/publication/state-young -america-databook.

2. Porter Stansberry, "The Corruption of America," Stansberry Investment Advisory, www.stansberryresearch.com/pub/reports /201112PSI_issue.html.

3. BBC News, "Buffett warns on investment 'time bomb,'" March 4, 2003, http://news.bbc.co.uk/2/hi/2817995.stm.

4. Charles Pierre Baudelaire, "The Generous Gambler," *Les Fleur du Mal: (The Flowers of Evil) and The Generous Gambler,* trans. Cyril Scott (Oxford, UK: Benediction Classics, 2012), 256.

5. Congressional Budget Office, *The Budget and Economic Outlook: Fiscal Years 2012 to 2022,* January 2012, xii, www.cbo.gov/sites /default/files/cbofiles/attachments/01-31-2012_Outlook.pdf.

6. "CBO: Obama Budget Creates $6.4 Trillion in New Deficits," Newsmax, March 16, 2012, www.newsmax.com/Headline /Obama-budget-deficit/2012/03/16/id/432800.

7. As of June 2012, according to data released by the Bureau of Labor Statistics.

8. In an unfettered free-market economy, artificial safeguards such as financial bailouts and stimulus programs are avoided so that financially fit enterprises normally survive economic setbacks and rebuild their businesses. Weak enterprises that cannot weather the downturn decline and often fail; the system allows them to fail. The capitalist system, if allowed to work as it is designed, would weed out businesses that fail to operate in ways that promote ongoing profitability. Unfortunately, two groups of players in Washington did everything possible to prevent that natural cleansing of our corrupted economic system. The bankers of the Federal Reserve System in concert with America's politicians failed to allow a natural recovery to take place without government interference. Instead, they took it upon themselves to determine which asset class would benefit from the transfer of the wealth of the world.

9. Talaat Khalil, "Home Prices in U.S. Cities Fall More-Than -Forecast 3.8%, Case-Shiller Says," HansaFx, October 25, 2011, http://hansafx.net/blog/?p=12830.

10. The rapid growth of future government spending is not primarily due to the cost of new programs but rather the cost of interest on the growing debt. In other words, it would not solve the problem to simply balance the budget. The federal government would have to begin running a financial surplus immediately and do so continuously for the next seventy years to prevent the danger-

ous debt–GDP ratio from rising. See Bruce Bartlett, "The True
Federal Debt," *New York Times,* January 3, 2012, http://economix
.blogs.nytimes.com/2012/01/03/the-true-federal-debt.

11. "The Widening Gap Update," Pew Center on the States, June
18, 2012, www.pewstates.org/research/reports/the-widening
-gap-update-85899398241.

12. "Obama's Budget Would Deepen Already Unprecedented Deficits," http://4.bp.blogspot.com/-gvllNObFGrs/TwCeFHHYZ-I
/AAAAAAAAJaQ/E0ax-SgMWdk/s1600/budget-create-deficits
-6004.jpg?utm_source=The+Lid+List&utm_campaign=846bd6c
269-RSS_EMAIL_CAMPAIGN&utm_medium=email.

13. Central Intelligence Agency, *The World Factbook,* https://www
.cia.gov/library/publications/the-world-factbook/index.html.

14. Milton Friedman, *Money Mischief* (London: Harvest Book/Har-
court Brace & Company, 1994), 49.

Chapter 3

1. David DeGraw, "The Economic Elite vs. People of the USA,"
AlterNet, February 17, 2010. www.alternet.org/story/145705
/the_richest_1_have_captured_america%27s_wealth_--_what
%27s_it_going_to_take_to_get_it_back.

2. Barack Obama's conversation with Samuel Wurzelbacher can be
found at "Obama–Spread the Wealth Around," Fox News. Watch
the video clip at www.youtube.com/watch?v=OoqI5PSRcXM.

3. John McCormack, "GE Filed 57,000-Page Tax Return, Paid No
Taxes on $14 Billion in Profits," *The Weekly Standard,* November
17, 2011, www.weeklystandard.com/blogs/ge-filed-57000-page
-tax-return-paid-no-taxes-14-billion-profits_609137.html.

Chapter 4

1. Alexis de Tocqueville, the French author of the 1835 masterpiece *Democracy in America,* examined nineteenth-century America's schools, farms, and businesses as well as its councils of government. He failed to find the reason for the remarkable strength of this new nation in those institutions. When he visited the churches and listened to the preaching of pastors "aflame with righteousness," he discovered the secret. When he returned to France, de Tocqueville declared, "America is great because America is good; and if America ever ceases to be good, America will cease to be great," www.sermonillustrations.com/a-z/a/america.htm.

2. Richard Lowry and Ramesh Ponnuru, "An Exceptional Debate," National Review Online, March 8, 2010, www.nationalreview.com/nrd/article/?q=M2FhMTg4Njk0NTQwMmFlMmYzZDg2YzgyYjdmYjhhMzU=.

3. John Winthrop, "A Model of Christian Charity," 1630, http://religiousfreedom.lib.virginia.edu/sacred/charity.html.

4. John Wycliffe, prologue to his 1384 Bible translation, emphasis added.

5. Abraham Lincoln, "The Gettysburg Address," November 19, 1863, http://showcase.netins.net/web/creative/lincoln/speeches/gettysburg.htm.

6. Quoted from the New Hampshire Constitution, www.lonang.com/exlibris/organic/1784-nhr.htm.

7. This is commanded by God: "And thou shalt teach them diligently unto thy children, and shalt talk of them when thou sittest

in thine house, and when thou walkest by the way, and when thou liest down, and when thou risest up" (Deuteronomy 6:7).

8. Quoted in Nancy Leigh DeMoss, *The Rebirth of America* (West Palm Beach, FL: Arthur S. DeMoss Foundation, 1986), 31.

9. The Treaty of Paris was signed in September 3, 1783, and brought international recognition to the national independence of the United States. The other combatants—France, Spain, and the Dutch Republic—signed separate agreements with Great Britain and individually recognized the United States of America as an independent nation.

10. During the summer of 1787 representatives met in Philadelphia to write the Constitution. The eighty-one-year-old Benjamin Franklin addressed the convention: "I have lived, Sir, a long time, and the longer I live, the more convincing proofs I see of this truth; that God governs in the affairs of man.... We have been assured, Sir, in the Sacred Writings that 'except the Lord build the house, they labor in vain that build it.' I firmly believe this," www.constitution.org/primarysources/franklin.html.

11. For more on these ideas, see R. J. Rushdoony, *The Nature of the American System* (Vallecito, CA: Ross House, 2002).

12. Historian John W. Whitehead wrote, "When the Reformation swept over Europe, it put the Bible in the hands of the people, revolutionized concepts of government and set the stage for the American Republic. With the influence of Samuel Rutherford, John Witherspoon and John Locke, the Bible became the basis of United States government and law." Quoted in DeMoss, *The Rebirth of America*, 35.

Chapter 5

1. See Peter Goodspeed, "Adapting the U.S. Forces for a Frugal Era," *National Post,* October 28, 2011, http://fullcomment .nationalpost.com/2011/10/28/peter-goodspeed-adapting-the -u-s-forces-for-a-frugal-era.

2. The numbers that help define the reach and power of the U.S. military are themselves hard to fathom. The U.S. Coast Guard is administered in peacetime by the Department of Homeland Security, but in wartime the Coast Guard reports to the Department of the Navy. The smallest branch of the U.S. military, the Coast Guard in 2008 had 40,000 active-duty personnel. The U.S. Army consists of more than 1 million soldiers: 543,000 active-duty, 350,000 in the U.S. Army National Guard, and 189,000 in the U.S. Army Reserve. The U.S. Navy has about 460,000 sailors; about 335,000 are active duty and 125,000 are in the Naval Reserves. The U.S. Marine Corps, formed as a brother service to the U.S. Navy, has about 198,000 marines; about 40,000 of them are Marine Corps reserves. In 2008, the U.S. Air Force had 400,000 personnel; about 330,000 are active duty, 74,000 in the U.S. Air Force Reserves and 106,000 in the U.S. Air National Guard. In 2008 the U.S. military accounted for about 3 million personnel; about one-half of them are on reserve status. See Kent Ninomiya, "What Is the Size of the US Military?" EHow, www.ehow.com/about_4595933_what-size -us-military.html#ixzz1l02MuEWr.

3. Military scholar Catherine Lutz of the Watson Institute for International Studies at Brown University has written that the global

reach of the U.S. military today is "unprecedented" and "unparalleled." *The Bases of Empire* (New York: New York University Press, 2009), 1.

4. Michael Mandelbaum, "In an era of tightening budgets, can America remain a superpower on the cheap?" *Washington Post*, February 17, 2011, www.washingtonpost.com/wp-dyn/content /article/2011/02/17/AR2011021704610.html.

5. Michael Mandelbaum, quoted in Peter Goodspeed, "Adapting the U.S. Forces for a Frugal Era," *National Post*, October 28, 2011, http://fullcomment.nationalpost.com/2011/10/28 /peter-goodspeed-adapting-the-u-s-forces-for-a-frugal-era.

6. Robert Gates, quoted in Goodspeed, "Adapting the U.S. Forces for a Frugal Era."

7. "Pentagon Successfully Tests Hypersonic Flying Bomb," AFP, November 17, 2011, www.space-travel.com/reports/Pentagon _successfully_tests_hypersonic_flying_bomb_999.html.

8. For more on this idea, see Hsien-Hsien Lei, "Beware of Genetic Bioviolence," Eye on DNA, www.eyeondna.com/2007/07/09 /beware-of-genetic-bioviolence.

Chapter 6

1. Rob Waugh, "The CIA wants to spy on you through your TV," Mail Online, March 16, 2012, www.dailymail.co.uk/sciencetech /article-2115871/The-CIA-wants-spy-TV-Agency-director-says -net-connected-gadgets-transform-surveillance.html.

2. Waugh, "The CIA wants to spy on you through your TV."

3. Waugh, "The CIA wants to spy on you through your TV."

4. Mike McAuliff, "Obama Signs Defense Bill Despite 'Serious Reservations,'" *Huffington Post,* December 31, 2011, www .huffingtonpost.com/2011/12/31/obama-defense-bill_n _1177836.html.

5. "President Obama Signs Indefinite Detention Bill into Law," American Civil Liberties Union press release, December 31, 2011, www.aclu.org/national-security/president-obama-signs -indefinite-detention-bill-law.

6. Dana Priest and William M. Arkin, "Top Secret America," *Washington Post,* July 19, 2010, http://projects.washingtonpost.com /top-secret-america.

7. Priest and Arkin, "Top Secret America."

8. Dana Priest and William M. Arkin, "A Hidden World, Growing Beyond Control," *Washington Post,* July 19, 2010, http://projects. washingtonpost.com/top-secret-america/articles/a-hidden-world- growing-beyond-control. A searchable database is available at the *Washington Post* website. Scrolling through the extensive research into the operations of the secret government, most of it hidden from any meaningful congressional oversight, will astound you. The searchable database is available at www.washingtonpost.com /topsecretamerica. It will astonish you even though Priest and Arkin's research covers only a fraction of the entire secret government operation.

9. See Priest and Arkin, "Top Secret America."

10. U.S. Department of Health and Human Services press release, January 20, 2012, www.hhs.gov/news/press/2012pres/01/20120120a .html.

Chapter 7

1. Richard Russell, "China," January 21, 2011, www.lewrockwell
   .com/spl3/russell-china.html.

2. "Cable 09Beijing1134, Media Reaction: U.S.-China-Japan
   Relations, U.S. Policy," http://wikileaks.org/cable/2009/04
   /09BEIJING1134.html.

3. Amanda Cooper, "Analysis: Yellow-BRIC road leads to mystery
   gold buyers," November 18, 2011, www.reuters.com/article/2011
   /11/18/us-gold-cenbanks-idUSTRE7AH1L620111118.

4. Porter Stansberry, "How and Why China Came to Dominate the
   Market for Gold," *Daily Wealth*, February 24, 2012, www.daily
   -wealth.com/1996/How-and-Why-China-Came-to-Dominate
   -the-Market-for-Gold.

5. Kopin Tan, "Enter the Yuan," *Barron's*, November 14, 2011,
   http://online.barrons.com/article/SB500014240527487038
   93804577024122523328762.html#articleTabs_panel_article
   %3D1.

6. Porter Stansberry, "Do You Have Money in These U.S. Banks?"
   http://pro.stansberryresearch.com/1202CHINAPT2/LOILN
   429/Full.

Chapter 8

1. Larry Elliott, "Decline and Fall of the American Empire," *The
   Guardian*, June 6, 2011.

2. See Michael T. Snyder, "Twenty Reasons Why the U.S. Economy
   Is Dying," *McAlvany Intelligence Advisor*, February 1, 2010, www
   .miatoday.com.

3. For more on these ideas, see Mark Steyn, *After America: Get Ready for Armageddon* (Washington DC: Regnery, 2009).

4. Peter Krauth, "The Last Five Minutes," *Real Asset Returns,* March 2012, http://moneymappress.com/category/trading-services/real-asset-returns.

5. Krauth, "The Last Five Minutes."

6. Katharine Comisso, "US reserves of rare earth elements assessed for first time," *New Scientist Physics & Math,* November 19, 2010, www.newscientist.com/article/dn19753-us-reserves-of-rare-earth-elements-assessed-for-first-time.html.

7. "Obama Mulls 80 Percent Disarmament of Nuclear Arsenal," Newsmax, February 14, 2012, www.newsmax.com/Newsfront/obama-Nuclear-Weapons-reductions/2012/02/14/id/429403. Russian president Vladimir Putin vowed to deliver an "effective and asymmetrical response" to the North Atlantic Treaty Organization's plan to create a missile-defense shield over Europe while thoroughly overhauling the Russian army's ability to confront modern threats. In response to NATO's antiballistic missile shield installed in the territories of European allies of America, Putin pledged to spend 23 trillion rubles ($770 billion) to strengthen the Russian army's military capabilities over the next ten years, the Kremlin's largest military spending increase since the end of the Cold War; see "Russian Prime Minister Vladimir Putin pledges more defense spending," www.foxnews.com/world/2012/02/20/russian-prime-minister-vladimir-putin-pledges-more-defense-spending/?test=latestnews#ixzz1myDk1F1Y.

8. See Min Zeng, "Fed's 'Operation Twist' Tangles Treasury Trade," *Wall Street Journal*, February 10, 2012, http://online.wsj.com /article/SB10001424052970203315804577211303042416034 .html.

9. Eric Sprott, Sprott.com, (www.sprott.com/markets-at-a-glance /unintended-consequences), citing an article by Ernest Scheyder and Jilian Mincer, "Analysis: Pension shortfalls a stark corporate challenge," Reuters, January 26, 2012, http://www.reuters.com /article/2012/01/26/us-corporate-pensions-idUSTRE80P037 20120126.

10. See Rebecca Christie and Peter Woodifield, "Europe's $39 Trillion Pension Risk Grows as Economy Falters," Bloomberg, January 11, 2012, www.bloomberg.com/news/2012-01-11/europe-s-39 -trillion-pension-threat-grows-as-regional-economies-sputter .html.

11. See Bryan R. Lawrence, "The dirty secret in Uncle Sam's Friday trash dump," *Washington Post*, December 28, 2011, www .washingtonpost.com/opinions/the-dirty-secret-in-uncle-sams -friday-trash-dump/2011/12/28/gIQArtWMNP_story.html.

12. See Michael Mackenzie, "China anticipates Fed quantitative easing," *Financial Times*, February 15, 2012, www.ft.com /intl/cms/s/0/27a221be-57e4-11e1-b089-00144feabdc0 .html#axzz1mSKyDrxw.

13. See Leslie Hook, "China gold imports from HK surged in 2011," *Financial Times*, February 7, 2012, www.ft.com/intl/cms/s/0 /d26cd2d6-518d-11e1-a99d-00144feabdc0.html#axzz1m H8V3yyg.

Chapter 9

1. See Jennifer Hodson, "Life-Settlements Industry Sees Growth," *Wall Street Journal,* February 5, 2009, http://online.wsj.com /article/SB123377502090848763.html.

2. Justin Brill, "Restrictions on Traveling and Purchasing Gold," *Daily Crux,* July 28, 2011, http://britanniaradio.blogspot .com/2011/07/dear-daily-crux-subscriber-u.html.

Chapter 10

1. Croatia is scheduled to become a member of the European Union in July 2013.

2. "What comes next after economy falls: Experts have United States of Europe rising from ashes," J. Farah's *G2 Bulletin,* November 21, 2011, WND, www.wnd.com/2011/11/369989.

3. See "What comes next after economy falls: Experts have United States of Europe rising from ashes."

4. Sanhedrin 97b, Talmud (London: Soncino, 1987).

5. See Grant R. Jeffrey, *Shadow Government* (Colorado Springs: WaterBrook, 2009), 132.

6. See Jeffrey, *Shadow Government,* 133.

7. *New York Times* Biographical Services (1979), vol. 10, 353.

8. Hans Tietmeyer, quoted in Arthur Noble, "The European Union," European Institute of Protestant Studies, August 28, 1999, www.ianpaisley.org/article.asp?ArtKey=eu2.

9. See Jeffrey, *Shadow Government,* 134.

10. Constant Brand and Robert Wielaard, "Conservatives Racing Ahead in EU Parliament Voting," June 7, 2009, http://seattletimes

.nwsource.com/html/nationworld/2009310031_apeuropean
elections.html.

11. See Diego Salazar Madrid, "Europe's lost generation: How it feels
to be young and struggling in the EU," *The Guardian,* January
28, 2012, www.guardian.co.uk/world/2012/jan/28/europes
-lost-generation-young-eu.

Chapter 11

1. See Charles Krauthammer, "The days of reckoning for Obamacare," March 23, 2012, *National Post,* http://fullcomment
.nationalpost.com/2012/03/23/charles-krauthammer-the-days
-of-reckoning-for-obamacare.

2. Tracy Winborn, "CBO Report: 'Obamacare' More Costly than
Promised," CBN News, March 19, 2012, https://www.cbn.com
/cbnnews/finance/2012/March/CBO-Report-Obamacare-More
-Costly-than-Promised. The Affordable Care Act was promoted
as a plan in which the cost over the first ten years would total less
than $1 trillion ($938 billion). President Obama crafted the initial two years (2010 and 2011) so that the startup costs would be
low. In fact, the true annual costs are not fully experienced during
the first four years. But over the following ten years, from 2013
to 2022, the costs will reach an amount that is almost twice as
large as the president stated (according to the calculations of the
Congressional Budget Office). The CBO states the true ten-year
cost will be $1.76 trillion, averaging $176 billion annually.

3. Stephen Moore, quoted in Patrick Hobin, "WSJ Economist:
Obamacare Costs Will Fall on Middle Class," Newsmax, July 2,

2012, www.newsmax.com/US/obamacare-cost-middle-class
/2012/07/02/id/444189.

4. Nick Gillespie and Jim Epstein, "Is There a Silver Lining to
the Supreme Court's Obamacare Decision? Q&A with *Reason
Magazine*'s Peter Suderman, June 28, 2012, http://reason.com
/blog/2012/06/28/is-there-a-silver-lining-in-the-supreme.

5. Peter R. Orszag, "How Health Care Can Save or Sink America,"
Foreign Affairs, July–August 2011, www.foreignaffairs.com
/articles/67918/peter-r-orszag/how-health-care-can-save-or-sink
-america.

6. Diane Cohen and Michael F. Cannon, "The Independent Payment Advisory Board: PPACA's Anti-Constitutional and Authori-
tarian Super-Legislature," *Cato Institute Policy Analysis,* No 700,
June 12, 2012, 7, www.scribd.com/fullscreen/97098735.

Appendix A

1. George Washington, "A Proclamation—Thanksgiving Day,"
October 17, 1789, as printed in *The Providence Gazette and
Country Journal,* www.wallbuilders.com/libissuesarticles.asp?id
=3584.

2. George Washington, Letter to the United Baptist Churches
in Virginia, May 10, 1789, www.pbs.org/georgewashington
/collection/other_1789may10.html.

3. George Washington, Inaugural Address to Congress, April 30,
1789, http://www.ushistory.org/valleyforge/washington
/earnestprayer.html.

4. George Washington, Farewell Address, 1796, http://avalon.law
.yale.edu/18th_century/washing.asp.

5. Thomas Jefferson, 1781, Query XVIII of his Notes on the State of Virginia. http://teachingamericanhistory.org/library/index .asp?document=529.

6. Thomas Jefferson, Letter to Dr. Benjamin Rush, dated April 21, 1803. www.let.rug.nl/usa/P/tj3/writings/brf/jefl153.htm.

7. Thomas Jefferson, quoted in Nancy Leigh DeMoss, *The Rebirth of America* (West Palm Beach, FL: The Arthur S. DeMoss Foundation, 1986), 24.

8. James Madison, Statement to the General Assembly of the State of Virginia, 1778.

9. John Quincy Adams, Address to the American Bible Society, http://record.americanbible.org/content/usa/presidential -wisdom.

10. John Quincy Adams, "Famous Bible Quotes from Famous People," www.basic-bible-knowledge.com/famous-bible-quotes .html.

11. Benjamin Franklin, "Benjamin Franklin's Request for Prayers at the Constitutional Convention," July 28, 1787, www.beliefnet .com/resourcelib/docs/21/Benjamin_Franklins_Request_for _Prayers_at_the_Constitutional__1.html.

12. John Adams, extract from a letter written to Thomas Jefferson on June 28, 1813, www.revolutionary-war-and-beyond.com /john-adams-quotations-2.html.

13. John Adams, "Message from John Adams to the Officers of the First Brigade of the Third Division of the Militia of Massachusetts," October 11, 1798, www.beliefnet.com/resourcelib /docs/115/Message_from_John_Adams_to_the_Officers_of _the_First_Brigade_1.html.

14. John Adams, letter to Dr. Benjamin Rush, August 28, 1811, www.revolutionary-war-and-beyond.com/john-adams-quotations -2.html.

15. Noah Webster, quoted in Nancy Leigh DeMoss, *The Rebirth of America* (West Palm Beach, FL: The Arthur S. DeMoss Foundation, 1986), 32.

16. John Jay, letter to John Murray Jr., October 12, 1816, www .godgov.org/id19.html.

17. John Jay, letter to Peter Augustus Jay, April 8, 1784, www .famousquotes.com/category/bible/9.

Appendix B

1. Andrew Jackson, quoted in William J. Federer, "The Rock Upon Which Our Republic Rests," *American Clarion*, June 8, 2012, www.americanclarion.com/8769/2012/06/08/rock-republic -rests.

2. Abraham Lincoln, quoted in Roy P. Basler, ed., "Reply to Loyal Colored People of Baltimore upon Presentation of a Bible," *Collected Works of Abraham Lincoln*, 9 vols. (New Brunswick, NJ: Rutgers University Press, 1953), 7:542.

3. Abraham Lincoln, First Inaugural Address, March 4, 1861, www .bartleby.com/124/pres31.html.

4. Abraham Lincoln, quoted in Rufus Rockwell Wilson, ed., *Intimate Memories of Lincoln* (Elmira, NY: Primavera, 1945), 22.

5. *Holy Trinity v. United States*, 143 U.S. 457, 1892.

6. Calvin Coolidge, Memorial Day Address, May 31, 1923, www .americanclarion.com/8365/2012/05/31/choice-grain-wilderness.

7. Franklin Delano Roosevelt, quoted at "US History Quotes About God and the Bible," www.usachristianministries.com /us-history-quotes-about-god-and-the-bible.

8. Harry S. Truman, "Address Before the Attorney General's Conference on Law Enforcement Problems," February 15, 1950, www .presidency.ucsb.edu/ws/?pid=13707#axzz1zzXdzkiM.

9. Dwight D. Eisenhower, "Remarks Recorded for the 'Back-to-God' Program of the American Legion," February 20, 1955, www .presidency.ucsb.edu/ws/index.php?pid=10414#axzz1zzXdzkiM.

10. Ronald Reagan, quoted in Rick Saccone, "America owes much to God," *Pittsburgh Post-Gazette*, February 7, 2012.

Appendix C

1. Richard W. Ziolkowski, "Electromagnetic or Other Directed Energy Pulse Launcher," U.S. Patent 4,959,559, filed March 31, 1989, issued September 25, 1990, http://patft.uspto.gov, search on the patent number.

2. Sharon Weinberger, "The Voice of God Weapon Returns," *Wired*, December 21, 2007, http://blog.wired.com/defense/2007/12 /the-voice-of-go.html.

3. Noah Shachtman, "When a Gun Is More Than a Gun," *Wired*, March 20, 2003, www.wired.com/politics/law/news/2003/03 /58094.

4. Michael Hanlon, "Run away the ray-gun is coming: We test US Army's new secret weapon," Mail Online, September 18, 2007, www.dailymail.co.uk/sciencetech /article-482560/Run-away -ray-gun-coming—We-test-US-army's-new-secret-weapon.html.

5. Winn Schwartau, *Information Warfare: Cyberterrorism: Protecting Your Personal Security in the Electronic Age* (New York: Thunder's Mouth, 1996), 183–88.

6. Andy Oppenheimer, "Mini-Nukes: Boom or Bust?" *Bulletin of the Atomic Scientists* 60, no. 5 (September–October 2004), www .andyoppenheimer.com/wp-content/uploads/2010/07/Bull -mininukes1.pdf.

Wondering about the end times?
Let Daniel answer your questions.

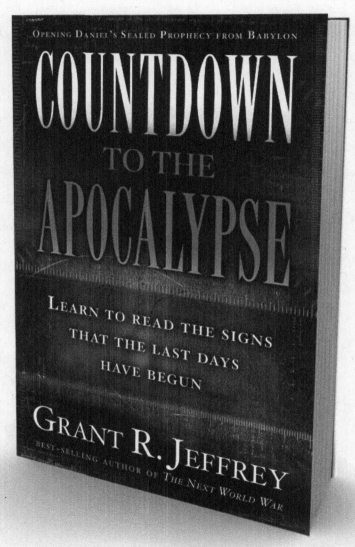

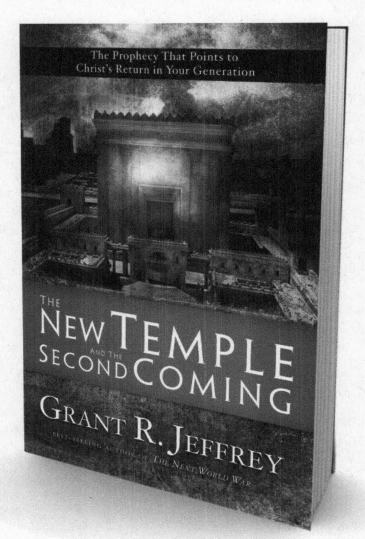